MW01062802

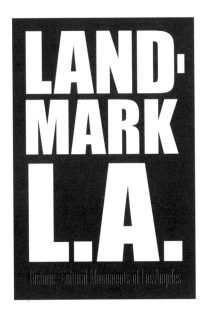

LAND-MARK L.A.

Historic-Cultural Monuments of Los Angeles

CITY OF LOS ANGELES
CULTURAL AFFAIRS DEPARTMENT

ANGEL CITY PRESS

LAND- MARK L.A.

Historic–Cultural Monuments of Los Angeles

Edited by Jeffrey Herr

Foreword by James K. Hahn
Mayor of the City of Los Angeles

LANDMARK L.A.: Historic-Cultural Monuments of Los Angeles
is a project of the Cultural Affairs Department of the City of Los Angeles.
www.culturela.org

Cultural Heritage Commission
Kaye M. Beckham, President
Michael A. Cornwell, Vice President
Mary Klaus-Martin
Johnny Grant
Holly A. Wyman

Margie Johnson Reese, General Manager, Cultural Affairs Department
Jay M. Oren, Historic Preservation Officer

Proceeds from the sale of this book support the Preservation Internship Program of
the City of Los Angeles Cultural Affairs Department.

LANDMARK L.A.: Historic-Cultural Monuments of Los Angeles is published by the City
of Los Angeles in cooperation with Angel City Press, Inc.
2118 Wilshire #880
Santa Monica CA 90403

LANDMARK L.A.: Historic-Cultural Monuments of Los Angeles
Edited by Jeffrey Herr
Copyright © 2002 by the City of Los Angeles
First Edition

ISBN 1-883318-29-7

Designed by Ardella Patterson
Production design by Amy Inouye, Future Studio for Angel City Press
Cover design by Amy Inouye, Future Studio for Angel City Press

10 9 8 7 6 5 4 3 2

LIBRARY OF CONGRESS CATALOGING-in-PUBLICATION DATA
Landmark L.A. : historic-cultural monuments of Los Angeles / edited by Jeffrey Herr.
    p. cm.
Includes index.
ISBN 1-883318-29-7
1. Monuments—California—Los Angeles. 2. Monuments—California—Los Angeles—
Pictorial works. 3. Historic sites—California—Los Angeles. 4. Historic sites—California—
Los Angeles—Pictorial works. 5. Cultural property—California—Los Angeles. 6. Los
Angeles (Ca.)—History. 7. Los Angeles (Ca.)—History—Pictorial works. I. Herr, Jeffrey.

F869.L865 A2 2002
979.4'94'00222—dc21
                    2002013537

The splendor and heritage of Los Angeles continue to amaze newcomers. From the Harbor to Little Tokyo, to the grand San Fernando Valley, the city's monuments tell great stories of the history of Los Angeles. That history is complex, impressive and ever-changing. Whether told through a natural rock formation that came to be known as Eagle Rock, a theater called El Capitan or the first cathedral in the heart of downtown, the stories communicated by buildings, monuments, nature's offerings and cultural curiosities add a visual and tangible view of the past that cannot be replaced.

Each time the Cultural Heritage Commission and City Council designate a new monument, another aspect of the legacy of Los Angeles–whether historic or cultural–is preserved. *LANDMARK L.A.,* based on the work of a great team of historians and photographers, memorializes seven hundred of the impressive icons that Angelenos encounter every day. These official Historic-Cultural Monuments depict the important aspects of Los Angeles, adding another level of understanding of what makes the city one of the greatest in the world.

There is a need for new thinking about the preservation and maintenance of these treasures, and with *LANDMARK L.A.,* the Cultural Affairs Department hopes to stimulate the public's concern for protecting the history that exists on the streets around them. Landmarks do not survive unless the public interest is clearly articulated and coalitions are formed to advocate support for preserving the city's heritage. In a place where the next Big Idea is born again and again, these monuments provide a constant reminder of the creativity that has always thrived here, as well as inspiration for continued ingenuity.

The Cultural Affairs Department is proud to offer *LANDMARK L.A.,* a fitting tribute to the heritage and future of the City of Angels.

MARGIE JOHNSON REESE
General Manager
City of Los Angeles
Cultural Affairs Department

48

270

101

102

194

10

430

2

47

85

38

126

56

213

CONTENTS

FOREWORD

The Cultural Heritage Commission had its beginnings in August 1962, when its initial meeting was held to stop demolition of what were to become the first five Historic-Cultural Monuments. Today, Cultural Heritage Commissioners continue to deliberate on recommendations for preserving historic buildings, analyze applications for new monument designations and confer monument status with confirmation by City Council. The Commission also approves permits for demolition or substantial alteration of buildings on the landmark list and may, with help of City Council, delay destruction or untoward alteration for as long as 360 days. The Commission envisions a place where historic resources are recognized not only as symbols of the past, but also as integral parts of daily life. Through revitalization and reuse, these resources will be alive with activity in the city's future. They will be places in which to live, work, play, worship and study.

The Cultural Heritage program defines a way of preserving the past in the "City of Tomorrow." In order for historic buildings to play a central role in the vitality of the city's diverse neighborhoods, preservation must reflect the multicultural nature and profile of Los Angeles. The Cultural Heritage Commission seeks to commemorate contributions of all Angelenos by recognizing and respecting their additions to the built environment. In so doing, the Cultural Heritage Commission fosters a greater appreciation for Los Angeles and all aspects of its heritage.

LANDMARK L.A., which shows some of the finest historic buildings and sites in Los Angeles, celebrates the past and represents the promise of the future. It is produced by the City of Los Angeles Cultural Affairs Department and is intended to help in the exploration of the Historic-Cultural Monuments this city has to offer.

JAMES K. HAHN
Mayor

PREFACE

For many people, the mere mention of Los Angeles conjures a mental image of a vast urban region filled with all that is new, a city without history. But within the 468 square miles that comprise the Los Angeles city limits are thousands of houses, miles of freeways, numerous monuments and parks, and countless public buildings that are rich with a past and links to the city's culture. Many of these symbols of "the Southland" are treasures in their own right, signs of what is truly unique about the city. In 1962, as a response to those who recognized the value of preserving the significant sites of a world-class city, the Cultural Heritage Commission was formed to help stop the demolition of Los Angeles's historic and cultural landmarks. Because of the Commission's work, more than seven hundred Historic-Cultural Monuments have been designated; those remarkable sites are pictured in these pages.

The Numeric Listing of Historic-Cultural Monuments, which is presented starting on page 420, chronicles an eclectic mix of icons that illustrate the rich cultural heritage of the City of Angels. But just as this vast metropolis sometimes stretches the definition of "city," the list often stretches the traditional connotation of the term "monument." While it includes a classic variety of public buildings, private residences, bridges and memorial markers, the list is also peppered with some non-traditional landmarks that help define the character of Los Angeles, past and present. Such a list must include the star-studded sidewalks of Hollywood, the Moreton Bay Fig Tree planted in West Los Angeles in 1875, the granite blocks on Bruno Street that were part of the city's first paved streets, the towers in Watts created by Simon Rodia and a host of other uniquely L.A. locations.

The impetus to officially preserve the historic landmarks and cultural assets of Los Angeles began in the early 1960s with the enactment of the Cultural Heritage Ordinance. It placed the city in the forefront of historic preservation, as there was no precedent in a major urban center of comparable size or economic importance; indeed Los Angeles had an ordinance governing cultural and historic preservation three years before New York's was instituted. The ordinance created the Cultural Heritage Commission, which was charged with making recommendations to City Council to designate historical and cultural monuments that would develop and preserve the history of Los Angeles, the state and the nation.

The process of designating a monument begins when a location is nominated either by the property owner or another interested party. After the Commission reviews the nomination application and decides to consider the property for designation, the commissioners visit the site, accept public comment and then vote to either recommend designation or reject it. Once recommended, City Council makes the final designation.

Monument designation is conferred on structures and sites significant in the city's history or buildings that are a prime example of a particular architectural style. Eligibility is dependent on how well the site has been preserved, including the retention of the original design and materials. Designation recognizes the significance of the site and is an indispensable preservation tool, encouraging the preservation of unaltered structures and the restoration of those that have been changed over the years. To preserve the complex fabric of Los Angeles's unique urban character, permits for proposed alterations or renovations to designated monuments must be reviewed by the city's preservation architect to guarantee compliance with the *Secretary of the Interior's Standards for the Rehabilitation and Guidelines for Rehabilitating Historic Buildings* (1976). When a new site is recommended by the Commission and approved by City Council, it receives the next sequential number on the list of Historic-Cultural Monuments that began with the first five landmark designations recommended on August 6, 1962, the Commission's first day of business.

LANDMARK L.A. is the Cultural Affairs Department's first complete pictorial book of the Historic-Cultural Monuments (HCM) that give Los Angeles its distinctive character. The photographs of the sites in Part 1 are organized by location, in chapters that reference general areas or neighborhoods, and each photo is labeled with its HCM designation number. A brief description of the monument is provided in the Numeric Listing of Historic-Cultural Monuments, with each site referenced by its HCM designation number. The reference Index beginning on page 481 will aid readers interested in locating sites by name and/or category (i.e., residences, parks, trees, bridges, signs, architect names, etc.). Regrettably, some of the designated monuments no longer exist. In a few lucky instances, the buildings were relocated, but more often these missing monuments were destroyed. Some were lost to natural disasters; many others were razed to make way for development. In these cases, the site has been commemorated with the designation and is prefaced with the words "Site of" in all references in this book.

With the exception of two, all the landmarks are within the boundaries of the city of Los Angeles. Manzanar (HCM #160), the World War II relocation center for persons of Japanese ancestry and the S.S. *Catalina* (HCM #213), both significant to the city's history, are not. Even for the native Angeleno, it is helpful to note that many areas thought to be a part of the city may not be within its actual borders. To cite two examples, while Hollywood is part of the city of Los Angeles, West Hollywood is not, and, although a large portion of the San Fernando Valley is Los Angeles, the city of San Fernando has its own municipal government. Sites in independent municipalities are not on the list of Historic-Cultural Monuments of Los Angeles.

Please note that many of the monuments listed in this book are private residences. Historic-Cultural Monument designation does not obligate the owner to accommodate public access. As readers use this book to enrich their knowledge of the historic and cultural resources of Los Angeles, they are reminded and urged to respect the privacy of all property owners.

Historic-Cultural Monument designation is essential to help preserve the varied aspects of the City of Angels. With lessons learned when the burgeoning growth of the post-World War II years caused the loss of important landmarks before they could be preserved, the implementation of the 1962 Cultural Heritage Ordinance has saved places important to the city's heritage. As additional buildings and sites are designated, the unique character of Los Angeles will continue to be preserved.

JEFFREY HERR
Arts Manager
City of Los Angeles
Cultural Affairs Department
August 2002

LANDMARK L.A. is divided into two parts. Part 1 features photographs of 700 monuments, organized by regions of the city of Los Angeles, and provides the Historic-Cultural Monument (HCM) number, the name of the monument and its address. Part 2, the Numeric Listing of Historic-Cultural Monuments, describes each landmark in order of its designation. For additional information and cross-references by topic, consult the Index beginning on page 481.

PART 1

The southwestern sector of the city, stretching from Crenshaw Boulevard to Los Angeles International Airport and Venice, includes an unusual variety of Historic-Cultural Monuments. Village Green (HCM #174), a 1942 urban housing complex in Baldwin Hills, was based on the City Garden Movement principles of the 1930s. Its superior planning is equaled in the remarkably well preserved Leimert Plaza (HCM #620). Designed in the late 1920s by the Olmsted Brothers landscape firm (sons of Frederick Law Olmsted, who designed Central Park in New York City), the Spanish Islamic influence of its axial plan makes it an ideal entrance to the adjacent retail stores. The cultural and architectural diversity of this area is exemplified in the Holiday Bowl (HCM #688), a quintessential 1950s Googie design. It afforded the local African Americans and Japanese Americans a venue in which to socialize and bowl twenty-four hours a day. Further west is Hangar No. 1 Building (HCM #44), constructed in 1929 at Mines Field. Now Los Angeles International Airport, it has been superseded by the recognizable space-age Airport Theme Building (HCM #570) that was erected in 1961, a mere thirty-two years later. North of the airport is the fantasy-come-true of Abbot Kinney who developed his dream city, Venice, California, using the Italian city of canals as his inspiration. The Venice Canal System (HCM #270), complete with arched bridges, drew tourists and residential development. However, by the 1930s, when the Venice Division Police Station (HCM #595) was built, some of the canals had already been filled and the neighborhood began to attract artists. Venice remains an art-friendly community, as is illustrated by Binoculars (HCM #656). The four-story sculpture by Claes Oldenburg and Coosje van Bruggen also frames the entrance to the office building designed by architect Frank Gehry.

18

595

174

44

Moss Photography

**HCM #532
Venice Arcades,
Columns and Capitals**
67-71 Windward Avenue

**HCM #502
Furthmann Mansion**
3801 Lenawee Avenue

**HCM #270
Venice Canal System**
Bounded by Venice
Boulevard and
Washington Street,
west of Abbot Kinney
Boulevard

**HCM #344
Institute of Musical Art**
3210 West 54th Street

344

502

270

259

688

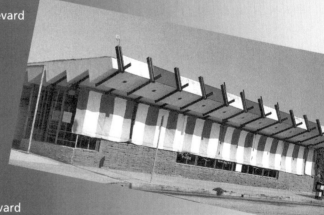

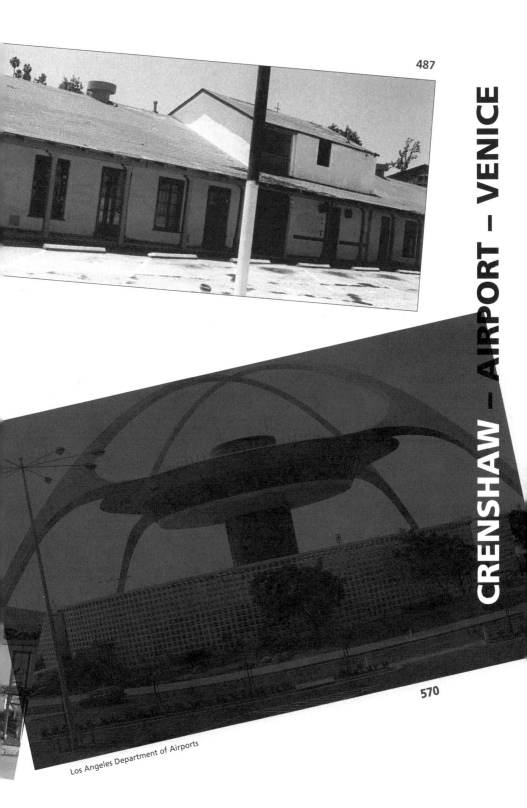

Los Angeles Department of Airports

656

HCM #656
Binoculars
340 Main Street

HCM #620
Leimert Plaza
4395 Leimert
Boulevard

HCM #624
**Lawrence and Martha
Joseph Residence
and Apartments**
3819-3827 Dunn Drive

624

620

679

HCM #679
Maverick's Flat
4225 South Crenshaw Boulevard

Los Angeles City Hall (HCM #150), erected in 1928, overlooks the downtown core and until the introduction of high-rise office towers, was the city's visual anchor. It is still a symbol of a city that spreads over 468 square miles. The architecture downtown is a rich mixture of styles and uses. St. Vibiana's Cathedral (HCM #17) was dedicated on April 30, 1876, and although no longer used for worship, is a vivid reminder of the religious influences prevalent in the early days of Los Angeles. The Bradbury Building (HCM #6) also originated in the nineteenth century. This 1893, five-story office building is significant for its glass-and-iron atrium. Its open-cage elevators and its ornamental balustrades and staircases have made the Bradbury Building a favorite motion picture location. The 1925 Fine Arts Building (HCM #125) is a Romanesque design featuring a two-story lobby lavishly surfaced with ornamental tile designed and produced by Pasadena tile-maker Ernest A. Bachelder. Nearby is the Central Library Building (HCM #46) by Bertram Grosvenor Goodhue. Its unique approach to the Spanish Colonial Revival style successfully demonstrates the broad interpretations of the design used throughout the city in both commercial and residential architecture. The Southern Pacific, Santa Fe and Union Pacific Railways opened an imposing and luxurious Union Station Terminal (HCM #101) in 1933, a design that successfully merges Spanish with Streamline Moderne. Still intact are a large number of Los Angeles's movie theaters. The 1927 Mayan Theater (HCM #460) is an exuberant interpretation of pre-Columbian design, illustrative of the exotic styles referenced in the movie palaces erected in the early twentieth century. Bordering downtown on the north is the San Antonio Winery (HCM #42), the only remaining winery in the city. South of downtown, the Vermont Square Branch Library (HCM #264) opened in 1913, the first permanent branch library building in the city and the first of six library buildings in Los Angeles funded by Andrew Carnegie.

3

HCM #3
Plaza Church
100 West Sunset Boulevard

HCM #5
The Salt Box
(destroyed)

HCM #4
Angel's Flight
4th and Hill Streets

5

4

125

HCM #125
Fine Arts Building
811 West 7th Street

HCM #150
Los Angeles City Hall
200 North Spring Street

HCM #137
Finney's Cafeteria
217 West 6th Street

HCM #131
Dunbar Hotel
4225 South Central Avenue

131

137

HCM #195
Oviatt Building
617 South Olive Street

HCM #138
Coca-Cola Building
1334 South Central
Avenue

HCM #159
**Ralph J. Bunche
Home**
1221 East 40th Place

195

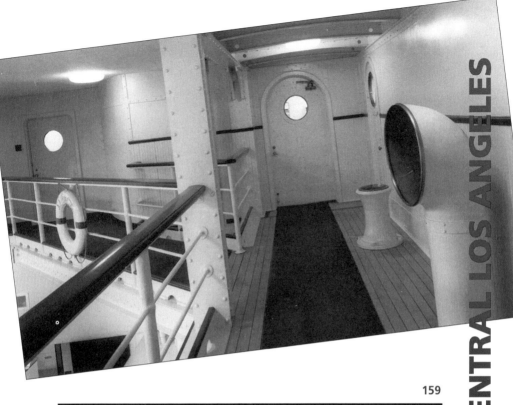

DOWNTOWN – CENTRAL LOS ANGELES

173

140

161

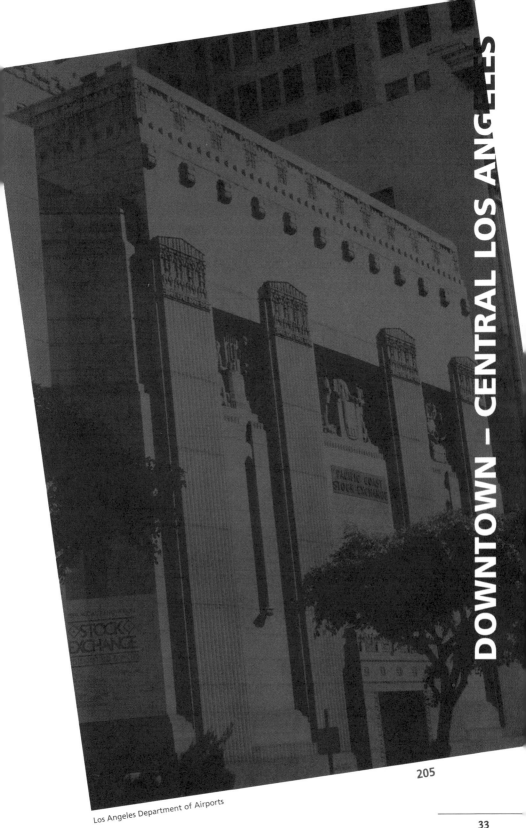

Los Angeles Department of Airports

HCM #225
Los Angeles Theatre
615 South Broadway

HCM #177
Subway Terminal
Building
417 South Hill Street

HCM #211
Granite Block Paving
Bruno Street between
Alameda and North
Main Streets

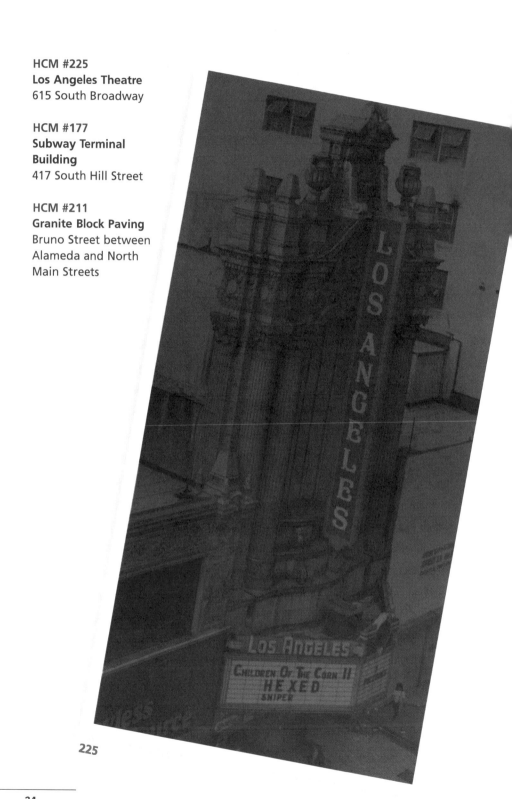

225

DOWNTOWN – CENTRAL-LOS ANGELES

HCM #196
Variety Arts Center
Building
940 South Figueroa Street

HCM #278
Title Guarantee & Trust
Company Building
401-411 West 5th Street

HCM #178
Herald-Examiner Building
1111 South Broadway

178

278

HCM #264
**Vermont Square Branch
Library**
1201 West 48th Street

HCM #271
**Farmers and Merchants
Bank Building**
401 South Main Street

HCM #255
The Original Pantry
877 South
Figueroa Street

HCM #281
Cathedral High School
1253 Bishops Road

264

281

271

255

286

HCM #286
Mayflower Hotel
535 South
Grand Avenue

HCM #299
Embassy Auditorium and Hotel
851 South Grand Avenue

HCM #294
Eastern-Columbia Building
849 South Broadway

294

DOWNTOWN – CENTRAL LOS ANGELES

HCM #288
Barclay Hotel
103 West 4th Street

HCM #312
Japanese Union Church
of Los Angeles
120 North San Pedro
Street

HCM #306
(Site of) Original
Vernon Branch Library
4504 South Central
Avenue

HCM #289
Fire Station No. 30
1401 South Central
Avenue

289

312

306

317

HCM #317
Young Apartments
1621 South Grand Avenue

HCM #300
Casa Camino Real
1828 South Oak Street

HCM #305
John Muir Branch Library
1005 West 64th Street

300

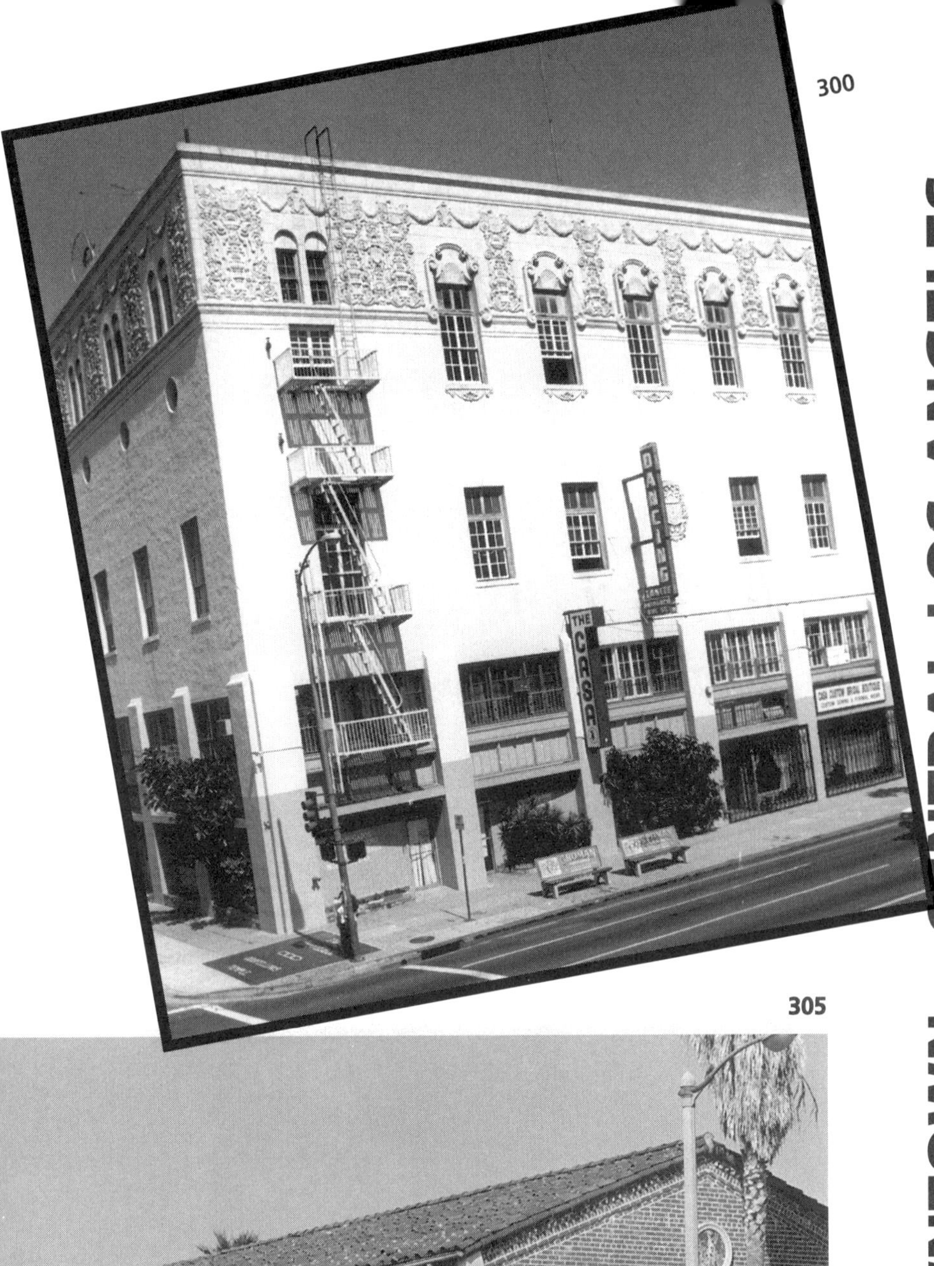

305

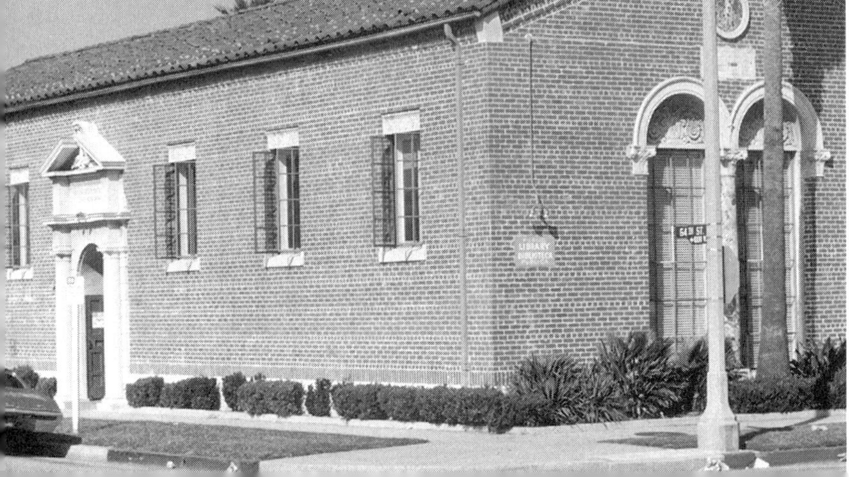

340

HCM #340
Standard Oil Building
605 West Olympic
Boulevard

HCM #323
**(Site of)
Church of the Open Door**
550 South Hope Street

HCM #313
**Los Angeles Hompa
Hongwanji Buddhist
Temple**
355-369 East 1st Street/
109-119 North
Central Avenue

HCM #352
Los Angeles Nurses' Club
245 South Lucas Avenue

352

323

313

HCM #347
One Bunker Hill Building
601 West 5th Street

HCM #357
**Boston Store/
J. W. Robinson's**
600 West 7th Street

HCM #345
**Harris Newmark
Building**
127 East 9th Street

347

357

345

386

HCM #386
Chapman Park Market Building
3451 West 6th Street

HCM #346
Coast Federal Savings Building
315 West 9th Street

HCM #356
Barker Brothers Building
818 West 7th Street

346

356

398

HCM #398
Pacific Mutual Building
523 West 6th Street

HCM #348
Fire Station No. 28
644 South Figueroa Street

HCM #460
Mayan Theater
1044 South Hill Street

HCM #385
**Title Insurance & Trust
Company Building and
Annex**
419 (Annex) and
433 (Building)
South Spring Street

385

ENGINE C⁹ N⁰28

460

HCM #526
Roxie Theater
512-524 South Broadway

HCM #358
Brock Jewelers / Clifton's
513 West 7th Street

HCM #355
Roosevelt Building
727 West 7th Street

HCM #354
Giannini/
Bank of America
649 South Olive Street

526

354

358

355

450

HCM #450
Tower Theater
800 South Broadway/
218, 224, 230
West 8th Street

HCM #480
**Spanish-American War
Memorial**
Pershing Square

HCM #459
**Hamburger's Department
Store**
801-829 South Broadway

HCM #449
Palace Theater
630 South Broadway

449

480

7ᵗʰ CAL. INF. U.S.V.

459

HCM #510
Residence
1157 West 55th Street

HCM #517
Residence
917 East 49th Place

HCM #472
**Rialto Theater
Building Marquee,
Box Office, and
Marble Entry Floor**
812 South Broadway

HCM #476
Belasco Theater
1046-1054 South
Hill Street

476

HCM #523
United Artists Theater Building
927-939 South Broadway

HCM #511
Residence
1100 West 55th Street

HCM #522
State Theater
Building
701-713
South Broadway/
300-314 West
7th Street

523

511

522

513

HCM #513
Southern California Edison Service Yard Structure
615 East 108th Street

HCM #518
Residence
1207 East 55th Street

HCM #580
Golden State Mutual Life Insurance Building #1
4261 South Central Avenue

HCM #524
Cameo Theater (formerly Clune's Broadway)
526-530 South Broadway

524

518

580

544

HCM #544
Irvine / Byrne Building
249 South Broadway

HCM #615
San Pedro Firm Building
108 North San Pedro
Street

HCM #525
Arcade Theater
532-536 South Broadway

HCM #651
Filipino Christian Church
301 North Union Avenue

651

615

525

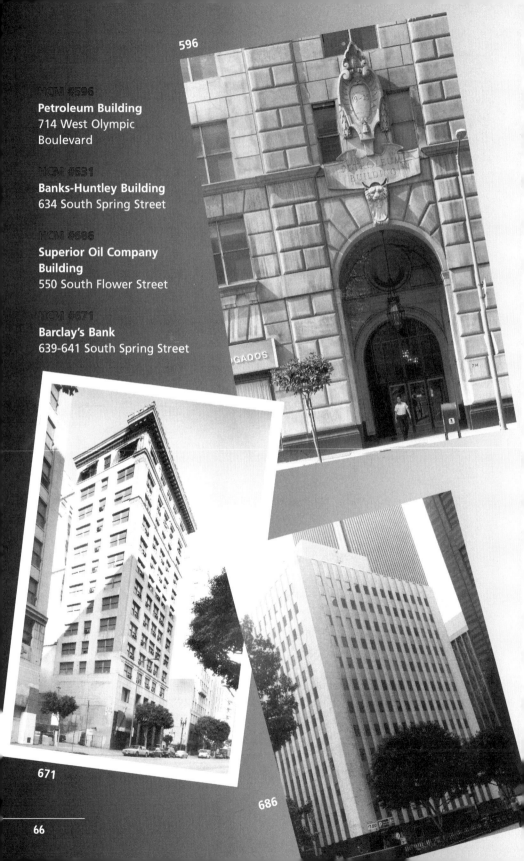

596

HCM #596

Petroleum Building
714 West Olympic
Boulevard

HCM #531

Banks-Huntley Building
634 South Spring Street

HCM #686

**Superior Oil Company
Building**
550 South Flower Street

HCM #671

Barclay's Bank
639-641 South Spring Street

671

686

6

HCM #6
Bradbury Building
304 South Broadway

HCM #16
(Site of)
St. Joseph's Church
218 East 12th Street

HCM #17
St. Vibiana's Cathedral
114 East 2nd Street

HCM #11
(Site of) The Rochester
Original location at
1012 West Temple

11

Los Angeles Department of Building & Safety

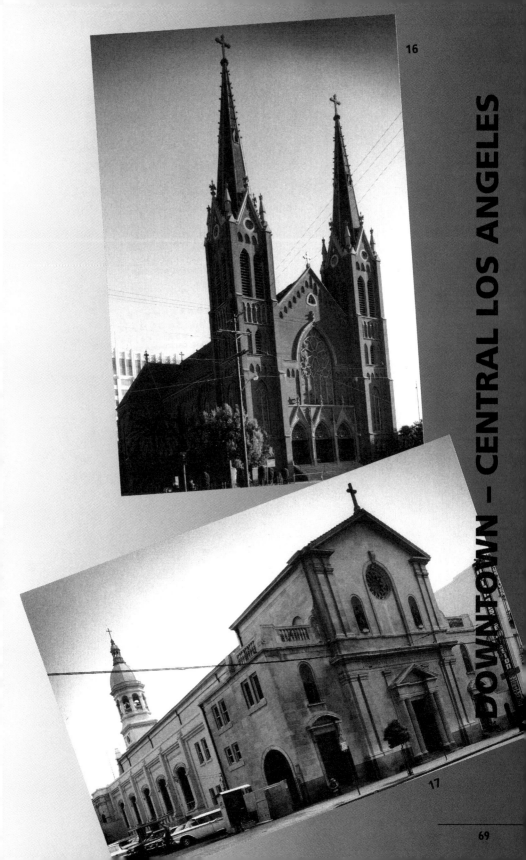

17

27

HCM #27
The Castle
(destroyed)

HCM #26
**(Site of) The First
Cemetery of
the City of Los Angeles**
521 North Main Street

HCM #42
San Antonio Winery
737 Lamar Street

HCM #37
Fire Station No. 23
225 East 5th Street

37

DOWNTOWN – CENTRAL LOS ANGELES

43

HCM #43
California Club Building
538 South Flower
Street

HCM #61
(Site of) Philharmonic
Auditorium
427 West 5th Street

HCM #60
Biltmore Hotel
515 South Olive Street

HCM #46
Central Library
Building
630 West 5th Street

46

61

60

HCM #71
(Site of) First African Methodist Episcopal Church Building
754-762 East 8th Street/801 South Towne Avenue

HCM #69
Los Angeles Athletic Club Building
431 West 7th Street

HCM #66
(Site of) St. Paul's Cathedral
615 South Figueroa Street

71

69

66

HCM #80
Palm Court, Alexandria Hotel
210 West 5th Street

HCM #82
**River Station Area/
Southern Pacific Railroad**
Between North
Broadway and
North Spring Street

HCM #99
Residence
1036-1038 South
Bonnie Brae Street

80

82

99

HCM #101
**Union Station Terminal and
Landscaped Grounds**
800 North Alameda Street

HCM #121
Garfield Building
403 West 8th Street

HCM #104
**Coles P.E. Buffet /
Pacific Electric Building**
118 East 6th Street

HCM #119
**Cohn-Goldwater
Building**
525 East 12th Street

DOWNTOWN – CENTRAL LOS ANGELES

121

HCM #64
Plaza Park
Bordered by Cesar E.
Chavez Avenue and
Alameda, Los Angeles,
Arcadia, New High
and Main Streets

HCM #219
Residence
1239 Boston Street

HCM #388
Edison Electric Co.
Los Angeles, No. 3
Steam Power Plant
650 South Avenue 21

Echo Park, with its attractive tree-lined lake, is one of the early developments adjacent to downtown. One of the highlights of this largely residential district with its eclectic mix of architectural styles is Carroll Avenue, a street noted for its Victorian houses like the Residence (HCM #52) designed by architect Joseph Cather Newsom. Although most of the houses in the vicinity are on their original sites, several of the Victorians have been moved from other areas. One example, the Residence (HCM #223) a Queen Anne confection with Eastlake and Moorish influence, was moved to East Kensington Road from Angelina and Boylston Streets in 1909. Nearby on Sunset Boulevard is Jensen's Recreation Center and Electric Roof Sign (HCM #652). Erected in 1924, this pre-neon incandescent sign features 1,320 bulbs and was restored in 1997. Adjacent to Echo Park is Elysian Park, home to Southern California's first botanical garden, the Chavez Ravine Arboretum (HCM #48), founded in 1893 by the Los Angeles Horticultural Society.

8

76

52

HCM #52
Residence
1330 Carroll Avenue

HCM #48
Chavez Ravine
Arboretum
Elysian Park

HCM #77
Residence
1320 Carroll Avenue

ECHO PARK

48

77

73

HCM #73
Residence
1329 Carroll Avenue

HCM #79
Residence
1344 Carroll Avenue

HCM #78
Residence
1324 Carroll Avenue

HCM #75
Residence
1355 Carroll Avenue

75

79

78

HCM #109
Residence
1325 Carroll Avenue

HCM #110
Los Angeles Police Academy Rock Garden
1880 North Academy Drive

HCM #166
Carriage House
1417 Kellam Avenue

109

110

166

191

189

176

190

HCM #190
**Residence and
Carriage House**
1411 Carroll Avenue

HCM #215
Bob's Market
1234 Bellevue Avenue

HCM #207
Residence
1334 Kellam Avenue

HCM #216
Residence
917 Douglas Street

216

215

207

217

HCM #217
Residence
1101 Douglas Street

HCM #218
Residence
945 East Edgeware Road

HCM #223
Residence
824 East Kensington Road

218

223

221

HCM #221
Residence and Carriage House
1347 Kellam Avenue

HCM #220
Residence
1343 Kellam Avenue

HCM #256
Mack Sennett Studios
1712 Glendale Boulevard

220

256

266

321

257

HCM #222
Residence
1405 Kellam Avenue

HCM #605
Old Fire Station No. 6
534 East Edgeware Road

HCM #504
Barlow Sanatorium
2000 Stadium Way

222

605

504

HCM #652
Jensen's Recreation Center and Electric Roof Sign
1700 Sunset Boulevard

652

Street murals are synonymous with East Los Angeles, and the area also contains a significant number of Historic-Cultural Monuments. East L.A. is connected to downtown by the 4th and Lorena Streets Bridge (HCM #265) built in 1928 by the city's Bureau of Engineering. This rare catenary-arched bridge also provides access to the Brooklyn Avenue Neighborhood Corridor (HCM #590), nominated for its symbolic association with the Jewish immigrants who ventured to Los Angeles from New York City in the early twentieth century and settled in this quarter. The earliest surviving Chinese-built structure in Los Angeles is in Evergreen Cemetery on North Evergreen Avenue. The twin ceremonial burners flanking a central altar of the Chinese Cemetery Shrine (HCM #486) were constructed in 1888. In nearby Lincoln Heights, with its lake within a park, is the Albion Cottages and Milagro Market (HCM #442). This 1875 complex housed laborers hired by the Southern Pacific Railroad and provided them with a market for food. Just 165 years later, the Streamline Moderne Fire Station No. 1 (HCM #156) was constructed. Lincoln Heights also benefited from the generosity of Andrew Carnegie in 1916 when the Italian Renaissance Lincoln Heights Branch Library (HCM #261) was erected.

102

97

54

144

145

HCM #145
Residence
3537 Griffin Avenue

HCM #265
Bridge
4th and Lorena Streets

HCM #263
Villa Rafael
2123 Parkside Avenue

HCM #156
Fire Station No. 1
2230 Pasadena Avenue

156

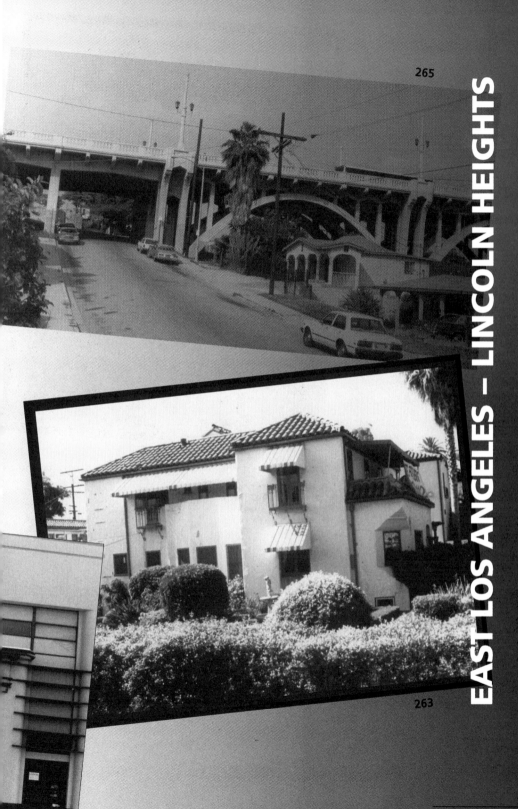

265

263

HCM #157
Residence
3110 North Broadway

HCM #153
**(Site of) Lincoln
Park Carousel**
Mission Road and
Valley Boulevard

HCM #590
**Brooklyn Avenue
Neighborhood Corridor**
Cesar Chavez Avenue
between Cummings
Street and Mott Street

HCM #442
**Albion Cottages
& Milagro Market**
1801-1813 Albion Street

157

442

153

590

HCM #384
Water and Power Building
2417 Daly Street

HCM #304
Malabar Branch Library
2801 East Wabash Avenue

HCM #443
Bowman Residence
2425 Griffin Avenue

HCM #396
Federal Bank Building
2201 North Broadway

384

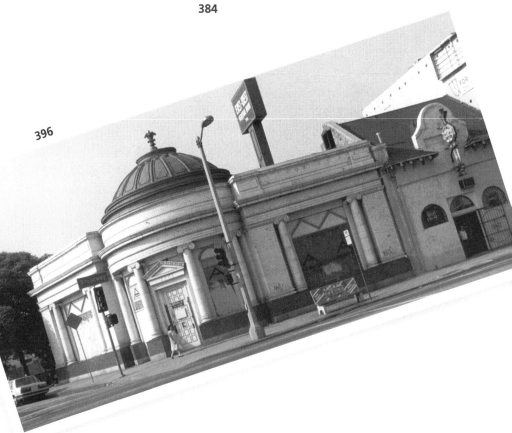

396

304

443

224

486

Sacred Heart Church
2210-2212 Sichel Street
2801 Baldwin Street

Lincoln Heights Jail / Los Angeles City Jail
401-449 North Avenue 19

Lincoln Heights Library
2530 Workman Street

468

261

EAST LOS ANGELES

HCM #533
Residence
2660 Sichel Street

533

One of the world's most recognized logos was born when the Hollywood Sign (HCM #111) was erected in 1923. Originally built by a real estate developer to advertise the residential development of Hollywoodland, the first sign's thirteen fifty-foot-high letters were outlined with four thousand light bulbs. Rebuilt several times, now only the renowned name "Hollywood" remains—sans light bulbs. In the streets below lies the Hollywood Chamber of Commerce's Hollywood Walk of Fame (HCM #194), more self-promotion inaugurated in the late 1950s. Embedded in the terrazzo sidewalks of Hollywood Boulevard and Vine Streets are more than 2,500 stars commemorating the names of motion picture, radio, television and recording celebrities. Here too are exotic movie houses such as Grauman's Chinese Theatre (HCM #55), which opened in 1927 with the premiere of Cecil B. DeMille's *The King of Kings.* Its forecourt is internationally renowned for the foot- and hand prints of motion picture stars that are pressed into the concrete. Crossroads of the World (HCM #134), a shopping center with an eclectic architectural theme, opened on Sunset Boulevard in 1936. Its centerpiece is a Streamline Moderne ship surrounded by shops in a variety of European Period Revival styles. Chateau Marmont (HCM #151), a hotel with a vivid history of celebrity guests, still thrives on the Sunset Strip, an area renowned in the 1940s for nightclubs such as the Trocadero, Mocambo and Ciro's, all now long gone. Hollyhock House (HCM #12) in Barnsdall Art Park (HCM #34) is one of the architectural treasures of the Los Feliz district of east Hollywood. Oil heiress Aline Barnsdall commissioned architect Frank Lloyd Wright to design a performing arts complex on the site she called Olive Hill. Never fully realized, the project resulted in Wright's first residential building in Los Angeles.

HCM #34
Barnsdall Art Park
4800 Hollywood Boulevard

HCM #12
Hollyhock House
Barnsdall Art Park
4808 Hollywood Boulevard

HCM #20
Two Stone Gates
Intersection of Beachwood,
Westshire and Belden Drives

34

20

12

33

58

HCM #33
Residence "A"
Barnsdall Art Park
4800 Hollywood Boulevard

HCM #55
Grauman's Chinese Theatre
6925 Hollywood Boulevard

HCM #58
**A&M Records Studio
(original Charlie Chaplin
Studio)**
1416 North La Brea Avenue

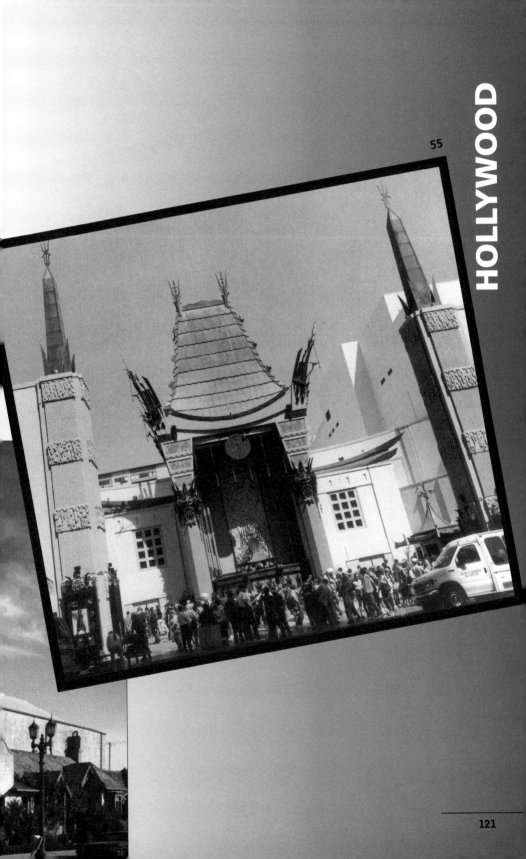

130

134

96

192

HCM #192
(Site of) Franklin
Garden Apartments
6917-6933
Franklin Avenue

HCM #151
Chateau Marmont
8221 West Sunset
Boulevard

HCM #175
Y.W.C.A. Hollywood
Studio Club
1215 Lodi Place

HCM #180
(Site of) Filming
of First Talking Feature Film
5800 West Sunset Boulevard

180

Courtesy Chateau Marmont

HOLLYWOOD

151

175

HCM #316
William Stromberg Clock
6439 Hollywood Boulevard

HCM #227
Janes House
6541 Hollywood Boulevard

HCM #193
Pantages Theater
6233 Hollywood Boulevard

HCM #234
(Site of) Taft House
7777 West Sunset Boulevard

234

HCM #535
Hollywoodland Granite
Retaining Walls and
Interconnecting
Granite Stairs
Upper Beachwood Canyon

HCM #243
(Site of) Garden Court
Apartments
7021 Hollywood Boulevard

HCM #235
Bollman House
1530 North Ogden Drive

HCM #246
Residence
1443 North Martel Avenue

246

243

235

HCM #277
Hollywood Masonic Temple
6840 Hollywood Boulevard

HCM #260
Edwards House
5642 Holly Oak Drive

HCM #248
First United Methodist
Church of Hollywood
6817 Franklin Avenue

HCM #247
Freeman House
1962 Glencoe Way

277

247

260

248

314

285

291

HCM #315
Villa Carlotta
5959 Franklin Avenue

HCM #421
Lake Hollywood
Reservoir
2460 Lake
Hollywood Drive

HCM #329
Chateau Elysee
5930 Franklin
Avenue

315

HCM #334
Security Trust & Savings Building
6381-6385
Hollywood
Boulevard

334

421

329

HCM #397
Roman Gardens
2000 North
Highland Avenue

HCM #441
Dunning House
5552 Carlton Way

HCM #406
Magic Castle
7001 Franklin Avenue

397

406

448

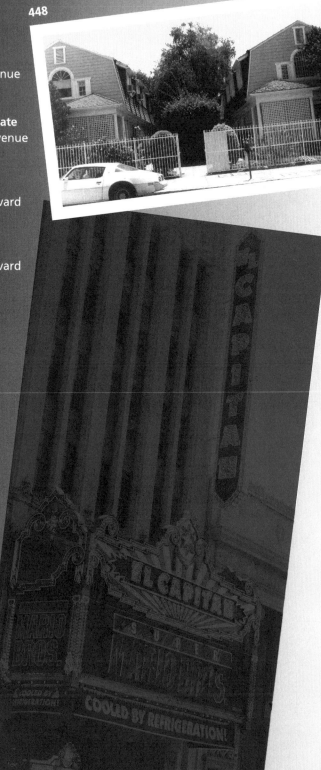

495

445

382

475

453

HCM #475
Highland Towers
Apartments
1920-1928 North
Highland Avenue

HCM #462
Hollywood American
Legion Post 43
2035 North
Highland Avenue

HCM #226
(Site of) Masquers
Club Building
1765 North Sycamore Avenue

HCM #453
Artisan's Patio Complex
6727-6733 Hollywood Boulevard

462

226

HCM #521
Taggart House
5423 Black Oak Drive

HCM #545
**Hollywood
Roosevelt Hotel**
7000 Hollywood
Boulevard

HCM #527
Residence
1437 North
Martel Avenue

HCM #390
Jardinette Apartments
5128 Marathon Street

521

390

545

527

HCM #559
13th Church of Christ, Scientist
1750 North Edgemont Street

HCM #579
**Wattles Park, Mansion
and Gardens**
1824-1850 North Curson Avenue

HCM #588
**Janss Investment Company
Uptown Branch Office Building**
500-508 North Western Avenue

HCM #572
**Warner Brothers
Hollywood Theatre**
6433 Hollywood Boulevard

572

579

588

HCM #597
Raymond Chandler
Square
Intersection of
Hollywood and
Cahuenga Boulevards

HCM #593
Max Factor
Make-Up Salon
1666 North Highland
Avenue

HCM #584
Egyptian Theatre
6706-6712 Hollywood
Boulevard

584

593

617

604

616

603

HCM #648
Withers Residence
2731 Woodshire Drive

HCM #630
Pierson Residence
3124 Belden Drive

HCM #666
**Taft Building and
Neon Sign**
6280 Hollywood
Boulevard

HCM #659
Pacific's Cinerama Dome Theatre and Marquee
6360 Sunset Boulevard

HCM #665
Hollywood Plaza Hotel and Neon Sign
1633 Vine Street

HCM #675
Villa Elaine
1241-1249 North Vine Street

HCM #664
Broadway Department Store and Neon Sign
6300 Hollywood Boulevard

664

675

HCM #301
Arzner/Morgan Residence
2249 Mountain Oak Drive

HCM #198
KCET Studios
4401 West Sunset
Boulevard

HCM #687
Tornborg House
1918 North Tamarind
Avenue

301

687

HCM #165
Fire Station No. 27
1355 North Cahuenga
Boulevard

HCM #194
Hollywood Walk of Fame
Hollywood Boulevard

HCM #463
Afton Arms Apartments   165
6141 Afton Place

HCM #336
Hollywood-Western Building
5500-5510 Hollywood Boulevard

336

194

463

673

HCM #673
The Outpost II
1851 Outpost Drive

HCM #689
**Philip Chandler
House**
2531 North
Catalina Street

689

Highland Park, bordering the Arroyo Seco, attracted noted Southwestern historian, Charles Fletcher Lummis, a journalist, photographer, author and archaeologist. In 1898, he built *El Alisal*, or the Charles Lummis Residence (HCM #68), a large house, mainly constructed by Lummis with arroyo stones from plans prepared by his friend, architect Sumner P. Hunt. Lummis also founded the Southwest Museum (HCM #283), a massive Mission and Spanish Colonial Revival structure, in 1903 to preserve artifacts of the native peoples of the American Southwest. It is the first museum established in Los Angeles and the oldest privately endowed California museum devoted to Native American culture. Across the Arroyo Seco stands Octagon House (HCM #413). Built in 1893 by Gilbert Longfellow, it is one of two eight-sided houses remaining in California and the only one in Southern California. It was moved to its present location in Heritage Square in 1986. Heritage Square is a mix of Victorian structures that have been relocated to save them from demolition. Highland Park's business district is the site of York Boulevard State Bank/Bank of America and Storefronts (HCM #581) founded by the residents in 1929. To the north is Eagle Rock (HCM #10), a natural rock formation that was noted by Spanish explorers for its distinguishing feature, the remarkably defined shape of an eagle in flight. When the town of the same name constructed the Eagle Rock City Hall (HCM #59) in 1922, it had only been incorporated for eleven years. Eagle Rock became a part of the city of Los Angeles the following year and its city hall was the first to be acquired by Los Angeles through annexation. Not far away is the Eagle Rock Women's Twentieth Century Clubhouse (HCM #537), built in 1915 by the women's philanthropic group with assistance from members' husbands.

HCM #22
The Palms-Southern Pacific Railroad Depot
Heritage Square
3800 Homer Street

HCM #40
Hale House
Heritage Square
3800 Homer Street

HCM #10
Eagle Rock
Northern terminus of Figueroa Street

HCM #65
Valley Knudsen Garden Residence
Heritage Square
3800 Homer Street

HCM #107
McClure Residence
432 North Avenue 66

HCM #62
Judson Studios
200 South Avenue 66

HCM #59
Eagle Rock City Hall
2035 Colorado Boulevard

59

107

62

106

108

274

105

HCM #105
Hiner House
4757 North Figueroa
Street

HCM #262
Residence
2700 Eagle Street

HCM #464
Fargo House
206 Thorne Street

HCM #143
Residence
6028 Hayes Avenue

143

262

464

492

392

HCM #541
Rev. Williel Thomson Residence
215 South Avenue 52

HCM #373
Arroyo Stone House and Arroyo Stone Wall
4939 Sycamore Terrace

HCM #413
Octagon House
Heritage Square
3800 Homer Street

541

373

413

412

287

614

282

529

612

HCM #529
Montecito View House
4115 Berenice Place

HCM #269
Mount Washington Cable Car Station
200 West Avenue 43

HCM #612
Birtcher-Share Residence
4234 Sea View Lane

269

HCM #379
Morrell House
215 North Avenue 53

HCM #374
G. W. E. Griffith House
5915 Echo Street

HCM #98
Mt. Pleasant House
Heritage Square
3800 Homer Street

379

HCM #378
Wheeler-Smith House
5684 Ash Street

378

HCM #245
Lincoln Avenue Church Building
Heritage Square
3800 Homer Street

HCM #691
**Carl C. Warden
Residence**
878 Rome Drive

HCM #284
**Highland Park
Ebell Club**
131 South
Avenue 57

245

691

284

179

581

377

482

HIGHLAND PARK – EAGLE ROCK

HCM #613
Scholfield House
4252 Sea View Lane

HCM #542
Swanson House
2373 Addison Way

HCM #416
Ziegler Estate
4601 North
Figueroa Street

613

542

416

HIGHLAND PARK–EAGLE ROCK

585

HCM #585
Occidental College Hall of Letters/
Savoy Apartments
121 North Avenue 50

HCM #470
Ivar I. Phillips Residence
4204 North Figueroa Street

HCM #394
Ernest Bent/Florence Bent
Halstead House
and Grounds
4200 Glenalbyn Drive

HCM #565
Charles H. Greenshaw
Residence
1102 Lantana Drive

565

470

394

503

380

338

569

HCM #400
Sun Rise Court
5721-5729 Monte Vista Street

HCM #437
(Site of) A. H. Judson Estate
4911 Sycamore Terrace

HCM #142
El Mio
5905 El Mio Drive

400

437

142

HIGHLAND PARK – EAGLE ROCK

376

HCM #376
**William U. Smith House
and Arroyo Stone Wall**
140 South Avenue 57

HCM #402
Ashley House
740-742 North Avenue 66

HCM #692
Dahlia Motors Building
1627 Colorado Boulevard

692

402

371

HCM #371
Tustin House and Arroyo Stone Wall
4973 Sycamore Terrace

HCM #283
Southwest Museum
234 Museum Drive

HCM #575
**Security Trust & Savings Bank,
Highland Park Branch**
5601 North Figueroa Street

283

575

369

481

395

556

HCM #375
Putnam House
5944 Hayes Avenue

HCM #411
Robert Edmund Williams House
840 North Avenue 66

HCM #418
(Site of) George W. Wilson Estate
616 North Avenue 66

HCM #404
Los Angeles Railway Huron Substation
2640 North Huron Street

375

411

418

404

HCM #393
Wiles House
4224 Glenalbyn Drive

HCM #611
Minster Residence
4163 Sea View Lane

393

611

HCM #370
**Herivel House and
Arroyo Stone Wall**
4979 Sycamore Terrace

HCM #582
W. F. Poor Residence
120 North Avenue 54

HCM #549
Highland Theatre Building
5600 North Figueroa Street

HCM #469
Ivar I. Phillips Dwelling
4200 North Figueroa Street

370

469

582

549

558

HCM #558
Department of Water and
Power Distributing Station No. 2
225 North Avenue 61

HCM #528
Dr. Franklin S. Whaley
Residence
6434 Crescent Street

HCM #562
Eagle Rock Women's
Christian Temperance Union
Home for Women
2235 Norwalk Avenue

HCM #554
La Paloma
369 North Avenue 53

554

528

562

HCM #372
Mary P. Field House and Arroyo Stone Wall
4967 Sycamore Terrace

HCM #550
A. J. Madison House
148 South Avenue 56

HCM #494
Kelman Residence and Carriage Barn
5029 Echo Street

HCM #564
E. A. Spencer Estate
5660 Ash Street

564

550

494

HCM #383
Residence
1203-1207 Kipling Avenue

HCM #536
Eagle Rock Playground Clubhouse
1100 Eagle Vista Drive

HCM #389
C. M. Church House
5907 Echo Street

383

HCM #537
Eagle Rock Women's
Twentieth Century
Clubhouse
5101 Hermosa Avenue

HCM #366
Latter House and
Arroyo Stone Wall
141 South Avenue 57

HCM #493
Casa de Adobe
4605 North Figueroa Street

HCM #539
J. E. Maxwell Residence
211 South Avenue 52

537

539

SOUTHWEST MUSEUM
CASA DE ADOBE

493

540

HCM #540
Piper House
326 North Avenue 53

HCM #483
J.B. Merrill House
815 Elyria Drive

HCM #461
(Site of) Meyers House
4340 Eagle Rock Boulevard

471

HCM #471
Argus Court
1760 Colorado Boulevard

Although Wilshire Boulevard extends from downtown to the Pacific Ocean in Santa Monica, its midsection between La Brea and Fairfax Avenues is known as the Miracle Mile. The commercial buildings have, to a large degree, retained their original façades. Two examples are the May Company Wilshire (HCM #566) and The Darkroom (HCM #451). Constructed in 1939, the structure for the May Company department store is distinguished by a four-story gold mosaic quarter-cylinder at its southwest corner, giving it a distinctive Streamline Moderne look. Of the same period, The Darkroom's 1938 façade, built to resemble an Argus 35mm camera, is an outstanding example of Programmatic architecture. Crossing the Miracle Mile is Highland Avenue with its Palm Trees and Median Strip (HCM #94). In 1928 the street's residents arranged for the city of Los Angeles to create and landscape the median strip at their expense. This area is also home to the Baroque-influenced 1929 Chapman Park Market Building (HCM #386). Designed in Churrigueresque style, it was one of the earliest automobile-oriented markets in the western United States.

HCM #508
Gilmore Gasoline Service Station
859 North Highland Avenue

HCM #183
(Site of) West Façade of the Pan Pacific Auditorium
7600 Beverly Boulevard

HCM #424
Apartment Building
626 South Burnside Avenue

HCM #81
Memorial Library
4625 West Olympic
Boulevard

508

81

183

424

HCM #94
**Palm Trees and
Median Strip**
Highland Avenue
between Wilshire
Boulevard and
Melrose Avenue

HCM #436
**Howard / Nagin
Residence**
146 South Fuller
Avenue

HCM #429
Apartment Building
601 South
Cloverdale Avenue

436

429

667

426

122

275

439

HCM #439
Apartment Building
450 South Detroit Street

HCM #332
Wilshire Tower
5514 Wilshire Boulevard

HCM #658
Harry and Grace Wurtzel House
926 Longwood Avenue

332

658

427

428

451

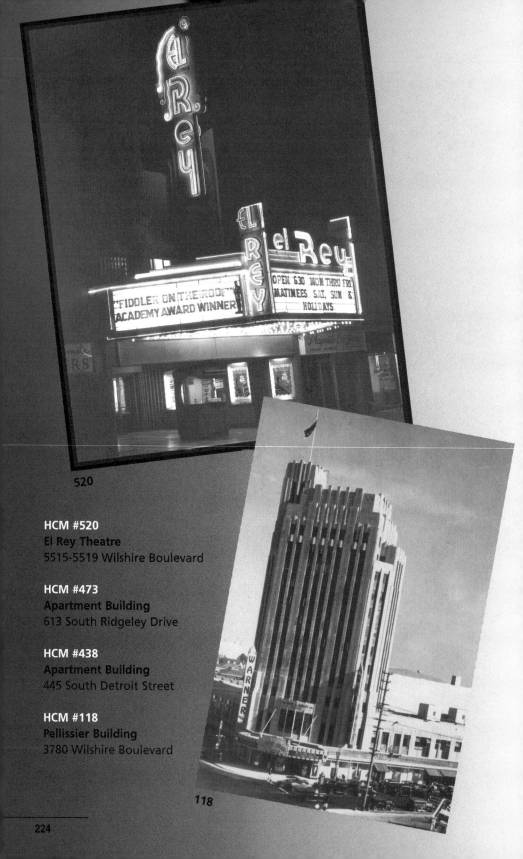

520

HCM #520
El Rey Theatre
5515-5519 Wilshire Boulevard

HCM #473
Apartment Building
613 South Ridgeley Drive

HCM #438
Apartment Building
445 South Detroit Street

HCM #118
Pellissier Building
3780 Wilshire Boulevard

118

473

438

566

430

543

425

HCM #425
Apartment Building
636 South Burnside Avenue

HCM #444
Octavius W. Morgan Residence
181 South Alta Vista Street

HCM #625
Thomas Butler Henry Residence
1400 South Manhattan Place

444

625

423

HCM #423
Apartment Building
607 South Burnside Avenue

The San Fernando Valley, once an immense agricultural area, is now an important residential, commercial and industrial sector of the city of Los Angeles whose history is integral to the city itself. The San Fernando Mission (HCM #23), the seventeenth church in the California mission chain, was founded by the Franciscan padres. Erected in 1797, the present church is a reconstruction of the one demolished in the 1971 San Fernando earthquake. Its convent, the largest adobe (mud block) structure in California, was completed in 1822 after thirteen years of construction and is still standing. Travelers on the El Camino Real received accommodations in this building, which, no doubt, contributed to the Valley's legendary reputation for hospitality. Historically significant civic buildings from the early twentieth century are also part of the cultural landscape. Bolton Hall (HCM #2) was constructed in 1913 of native stone for the purpose of housing a community center. The Valley Municipal Building (HCM #202), now Van Nuys City Hall, was erected in 1932 and immediately became an easily identified landmark. Faith Bible Church (HCM #152), first known as the Norwegian Lutheran Church, is a Gothic structure that was built in 1917. Historic residential structures in the San Fernando Valley range from The Magnolia (HCM #293), a late 1920s Spanish Colonial home that includes a detached garage with chauffeur's quarters, to multi-family structures. Rudolph Schindler's Laurelwood Apartments (HCM #228) were constructed in 1948 concurrently with the erection of Chase Knolls Garden Apartments (HCM #683). The latter, designed by Heth Wharton, was created following the City Garden Movement principles with pedestrian paths around an existing knoll and a stand of deodar cedar. The landscape design, especially the mature trees, is an integral part of Chase Knolls and one that sets it apart from similar projects.

HCM #638

El Paradiso
11468 Dona Cecilia Drive

HCM #141

Chatsworth Reservoir Kiln Site
Southeasterly from the intersection of Woolsey Canyon Road and Valley Circle Boulevard

638

HCM #573

El Portal Theater
5265-5271 Lankershim Boulevard

HCM #488

Canoga Park Southern Pacific Railroad Station
21355 Sherman Way

488

141

573

HCM #135
Canoga Mission Gallery
23130 Sherman Way

HCM #622
Taft House and
Landscaping
16745 San Fernando
Mission Boulevard

HCM #204
Lederer Residence and
Immediate Environs
23134 Sherman Way

HCM #644
Stone House
8642 Sunland Boulevard

135

644

622

204

181

31

1

290

HCM #290
La Reina Theater
14626 Ventura Boulevard

HCM #132
**Stoney Point
Outcroppings**
North Chatsworth

HCM #7
Andres Pico Adobe
10940 Sepulveda Boulevard

HCM #14
**Chatsworth Community
Church**
22601 Lassen Street

14

132

7

32

HCM #32
St. Saviour's Chapel
Harvard School
3700 Coldwater Canyon
Avenue

HCM #24
(Site of) Oak Tree
Louise Avenue 210 feet
south of Ventura Boulevard

HCM #50
Mission Wells and
The Settling Basin
Havana and Bleeker Streets

50

24

HCM #152
Faith Bible Church
18531 Gresham Street

HCM #49
76 Mature Olive Trees
Lining both sides of Lassen Street between Topanga
Canyon Boulevard and Farralone Avenue

HCM #184
**Tower of
Wooden Pallets**
15357 Magnolia
Boulevard

152

184

201

29

629

SAN FERNANDO VALLEY

HCM #63
McGroarty Home
7570 McGroarty Terrace

HCM #41
144 Deodar Trees
White Oak Avenue
between San Fernando
Mission Boulevard and
San Jose Street

HCM #683
Chase Knolls Garden Apartments
13401 Riverside Drive

HCM #23
San Fernando Mission
15151 San Fernando
Mission Boulevard

63

23

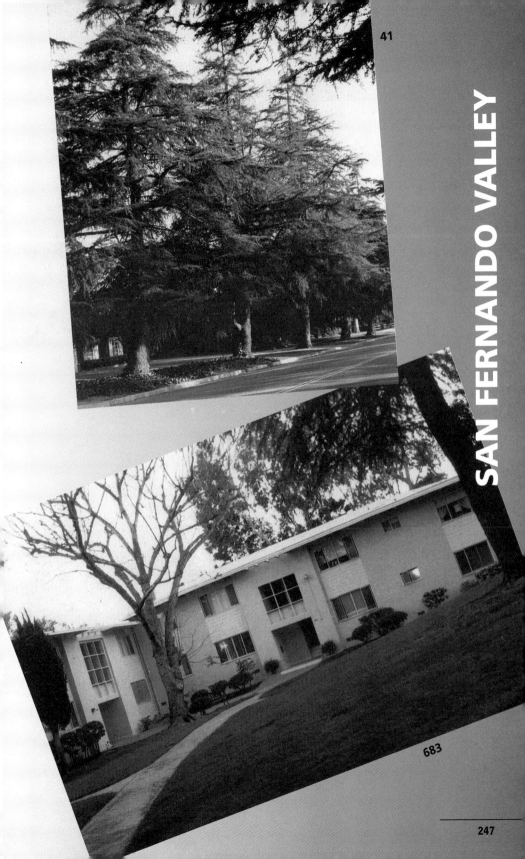

SAN FERNANDO VALLEY

683

HCM #133
**Minnie Hill Palmer
Residence**
Chatsworth Park South

HCM #484
Oakridge
18650 Devonshire Street

HCM #93
Pepper Trees
Canoga Avenue from
Ventura Boulevard
south to Saltillo
Street

133

93

199

HCM #199
David Familian Chapel of Temple Adat Ari El
5540 Laurel Canyon Boulevard

HCM #2
Bolton Hall
10116 Commerce Avenue

HCM #645
Harvester Farms
22049 Devonshire Street

HCM #293
The Magnolia
13242 Magnolia Boulevard

293

645

HCM #9
Shadow Ranch
22633 Vanowen Street

HCM #232
Department of Water and Power Building
5108 Lankershim Boulevard

HCM #586
San Fernando Pioneer Memorial Cemetery
14400 Foothill Boulevard

9

586

HCM #700
Canoga Park Branch Library
7260 Owensmouth Avenue

HCM #92
Old Stage Coach Trail Property
55 acres lying immediately south
of Chatsworth Park South

HCM #203
Baird House
14603 Hamlin Street

700

SAN FERNANDO VALLEY

203

228

HCM #228
Laurelwood Apartments
11833-11837 Laurelwood Drive

HCM #405
Pacific Electric Picover Railway Station
16710 Sherman Way

HCM #302
Amelia Earhart / North Hollywood Branch Library
5211 North Tujunga Avenue

302

Stan Cline (Artist's rendering)

405

HCM #172
Stonehurst Recreation Center Building
9901 Dronfield Avenue

172

Italian immigrant Simon Rodia began construction of what would be a lifelong obsession, the whimsical structures now internationally known as the Towers of Simon-Rodia (HCM #15), or colloquially as Watts Towers. Built in Watts between 1921 and 1954, the three towers and surrounding structures are decorated with broken bits of glass, pottery and other found objects set in concrete over a metal framework. Nearby is Watts Station (HCM #36), an early twentieth-century wood-frame depot representative of those that once existed in the towns surrounding Los Angeles in the early 1900s. The Wilmington and San Pedro areas, located near the harbor, are historically rich in cultural monuments. One of the area's earliest structures is Drum Barracks Officers' Quarters (HCM #21). This Italianate building housed the officers of Camp Drum, the United States Army headquarters for California, Arizona and New Mexico during the Civil War. Named in honor of General Richard Coulter Drum, commander of the Army's Department of the Far West, it was a sixty-acre military garrison constructed to protect the West from becoming a Confederate stronghold. Nearby is the General Phineas Banning Residence (HCM #25), an 1864 Greek Revival mansion built by the founder of Wilmington, California. In San Pedro, the Muller House (HCM #253), the circa 1899 Colonial Revival home of local shipwright William Muller, overlooks the harbor. Looking out to sea is Battery Osgood-Farley (HCM #515), a massive concrete bunker built in 1919 as part of the United States's coastal artillery defense and manned through 1944. Nearby, in Angel's Gate Park, the Korean Bell and Belfry of Friendship (HCM #187) was a gift from the people of the Republic of Korea in commemoration of the United States Bicentennial. The bell was patterned after the largest Asian bell in existence, the eighth-century bell of King Songdok.

HCM #15
Towers of Simon Rodia
(Watts Towers)
1765 East 107th Street

HCM #53
St. Peter's Episcopal Church
Harbor View Memorial Park
2330 South Grand Avenue

HCM #21
Drum Barracks and
Officers' Quarters
1052 Banning Boulevard

HCM #187
Korean Bell and
Belfry of Friendship
Angel's Gate Park
Gaffey and 37th Streets

187

53

21

47

HCM #47
St. John's Episcopal Church
1537 Neptune Avenue

HCM #36
Watts Station
1686 East 103rd Street

HCM #25
**General Phineas Banning
Residence**
401 East "M" Street

HCM #146
**Municipal Ferry Building
(Los Angeles Maritime Museum)**
Berth 84, foot of 6th Street

146

249

154

252

HCM #252
Harbor View House
921 Beacon Street

HCM #171
(Site of) Timms' Landing
San Pedro Harbor

HCM #186
Morgan House
437 West 9th Street

HCM #188
U.S.S. *Los Angeles* Naval Monument
John S. Gibson, Jr. Park
Harbor Boulevard between
5th and 6th Streets

188

186

571

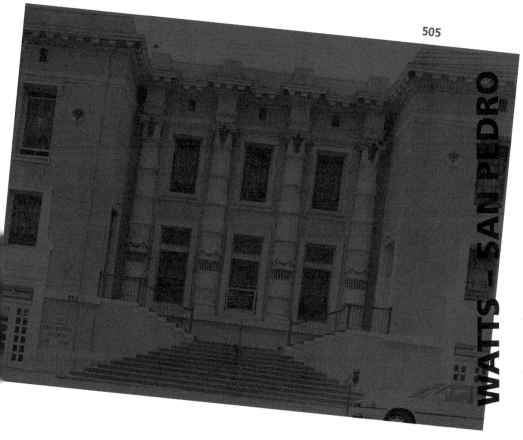

509

HCM #253
Muller House
1542 Beacon Street

HCM #514
Residence
383 10th Street

HCM #308
Wilmington Branch Library
309 West Opp Street

HCM #342
Masonic Temple
227 North Avalon
Boulevard

253

342

WATTS / SAN PEDRO

BIBLIOTECA
Del Pueblo De Wilmington

308

HCM #414
Wilmington Cemetery
605 East "O" Street

HCM #557
(Site of) Wilbur F.
Wood House
4026 Bluff Place

HCM #515
Battery Osgood-Farley,
Fort MacArthur
Upper Reservation
3601 Gaffey Street

414

515

557

HCM #147
James H. Dodson Residence
859 West 13th Street

147

The hills of Silver Lake, with their panoramas of Silver Lake and Ivanhoe Reservoirs (HCM #422), are home to a number of Modernist and Period Revival structures. The VDL Research House (HCM #640) by Richard Neutra was built in 1932 and reconstructed by him and his son Dion in 1963 after it was destroyed by fire. Neutra built several residences in the Silver Lake hills and worked out of the nearby Neutra Office Building (HCM #676). The reservoirs, still in use, were built in 1906 and at that time could supply the city with water for twenty days. Dominated by the Art Deco Griffith Observatory (HCM #168) in Griffith Park, Los Feliz is significant for its architecture and archaeological remains. The Gabrieleño Indian Site (HCM #112) was discovered at the mouth of Fern Dell Canyon and helped document the activity of these Native Americans in Southern California. The Los Feliz Heights Steps (HCM #657) include concrete fountains, benches, planters, retaining walls and metal railings. They were installed in 1924 during the development of the area to provide residents with easy access to hillside streets. The "Father of the Los Angeles Municipal Water System" was honored in 1940 with the dedication of the William Mulholland Memorial Fountain (HCM #162). Mulholland was chiefly responsible for the construction of the California Aqueduct that brought enough water to the Los Angeles basin to allow for population expansion.

SILVER LAKE – LOS FELIZ

124

112

123

136

HCM #136
St. Mary of the Angels Church
4510 Finley Avenue

HCM #126
Franklin Avenue Bridge
Franklin Avenue at
St. George Street

HCM #164
Glendale-Hyperion Bridge
Golden State Freeway
and Riverside Drive
between Ettrick Street
and Glenfeliz Boulevard

HCM #149
Ennis House
2607 Glendower Avenue

149

164

401

168

322

236

162

HCM #162
William Mulholland
Memorial Fountain
Los Feliz Boulevard and
Riverside Drive

HCM #343
Avocado Trees
4400 Block of Avocado
Street

HCM #474
The Little Nugget
Travel Town,
Griffith Park

337

HCM #337
Engine Company No. 56
2838 Rowena Avenue

343

474

HCM #891

Canfield-Moreno Estate
1923 Micheltorena Street

HCM #163

(Site of) First Walt Disney Studio
2725 Hyperion Avenue

HCM #353

Monterey Apartments
4600 Los Feliz Boulevard

391

163

353

HCM #657
Los Feliz Heights Steps
Cromwell Avenue, Bonvue
Avenue, Glencairn Road,
Bryn Mawr Road, and
Glendower Avenue

HCM #676
Neutra Office Building
2379 Glendale Boulevard

HCM #640
VDL Research House
2300 Silver Lake Boulevard

HCM #592
**Philosophical Research
Society, Inc.**
3910 Los Feliz Boulevard

657

592

640

422

553

699

HCM #699
August House
1664 Maltman Avenue

HCM #67
Cedar Trees
Los Feliz Boulevard
between Riverside Drive
and Western Avenue

67

One of the most prestigious residential areas in early twentieth-century Los Angeles was the West Adams district. The enclave that includes St. James Place and neighboring Chester Place, location of the Doheny Mansion (HCM #30), still retains many of the original opulent homes of the era. Mansions in various architectural styles such as the Chateau Revival Rindge House (HCM #95) were erected along West Adams Boulevard. William Andrews Clark's estate bordered the boulevard and his Italian Renaissance William Andrews Clark Memorial Library (HCM #28), now belonging to the University of California, Los Angeles, is the repository for his collection of primarily seventeenth-, eighteenth- and nineteenth-century English books and manuscripts. Houses of worship, such as Second Church of Christ, Scientist of Los Angeles (HCM #57), Saint Sophia Cathedral (HCM #120), St. Vincent De Paul Church (HCM #90) or the First African Methodist Episcopal Zion Cathedral and Community Center (HCM #341), are familiar sights. More modest but historically significant is the Residence of William Grant Still (HCM #169), an African American conductor and gifted composer. It is not surprising that Rosedale Cemetery (HCM #330), opened in 1884 and one of the first cemeteries in Los Angeles, is the site of many pioneer-family burials and important funerary architecture.

113

HCM #113
Young's Market Building
1610 West 7th Street

HCM #72
**Automobile Club of
Southern California**
2601 South Figueroa Street

HCM #349
Fire Station No. 18
2616 South Hobart Boulevard

HCM #35
**Birthplace of
Adlai E. Stevenson**
2639 Monmouth Avenue

35

72

349

28

HCM #28
**William Andrews Clark
Memorial Library**
2520 Cimarron Street

HCM #574
Pierce Brothers Mortuary
714 West Washington
Boulevard

HCM #127
Exposition Club House
3990 South Menlo Avenue

HCM #85
Gilbert Residence
1333 Alvarado Terrace

85

574

127

57

HCM #57

**Second Church Of Christ
Scientist Of Los Angeles**
948 West Adams Boulevard

HCM #95

Rindge House
2263 South Harvard Boulevard

HCM #280

Villa Maria
2425 South Western Avenue

HCM #272

Peet House
1139 South Harvard Boulevard

272

230

120

HCM #120
Saint Sophia Cathedral
1324 South Normandie Avenue

HCM #498
Lois Ellen Arnold Residence
1978 Estrella Avenue

HCM #170
Paul R. Williams Residence
1690 Victoria Avenue

HCM #677
Horatio Cogswell House
1244 South Van Ness Avenue

677

170

208

627

560

607

HCM #128
Hancock Memorial Museum
University of Southern California, University Avenue at Childs Way

HCM #185
(Site of) President's House, Pepperdine University
7851 Budlong Avenue

HCM #457
Freeman G. Teed House
2365 Scarff Street

Courtesy of Hancock Memorial Museum

128

185

Pepperdine University Archive

457

548

84

420

30

HCM #662
Perrine House
2229 South Gramercy Place

HCM #87
Raphael Residence
1353 Alvarado Terrace

HCM #331
Pacific Bell Building
2755 West 15th Street

662

87

331

117

HCM #117
Residence
2218 South Harvard
Boulevard

HCM #501
Michael Shannon Residence
1970 Bonsallo Avenue

HCM #661
Rives Mansion
1130 South Westchester Place

HCM #350
Ecung-Ibbetson House
and Moreton Bay Fig Tree
1190 West Adams Boulevard

350

501

661

HCM #90
St. Vincent De Paul Church
621 West Adams Boulevard

HCM #88
Kinney-Everhardy House
1401 Alvarado Terrace

HCM #479
Dr. Grandville MacGowan Home
3726 West Adams Boulevard

90

88

479

240

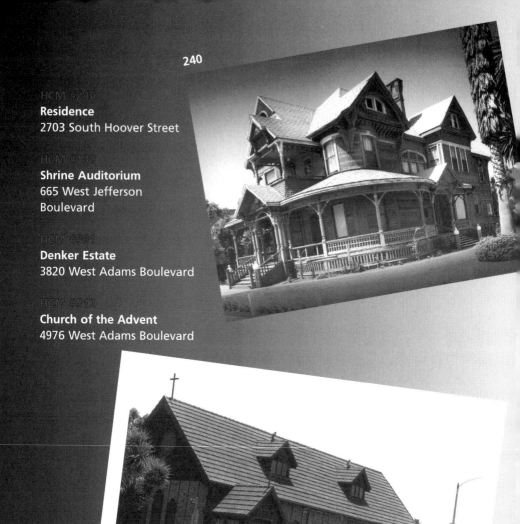

512

591

HCM #489
Richard H. Alexander Residence
2119 Estrella Avenue

HCM #307
Washington Irving Branch Library
1803 South Arlington Avenue

HCM #672
Percy H. Clark Residence
2639 South Van
Buren Place

489

307

672

89

HCM #89
Central Spanish Seventh-Day Adventist Church
1366 South Alvarado Street

HCM #410
Distribution Station No. 31
1035 West 24th Street

HCM #210
Terrace Park and Powers Place
Powers Place and 14th Street

HCM #600
Lucien and Blanche Gray Residence
2515 4th Avenue

600

410

210

499

408

598

419

HCM #295
A. E. Kelly Residence
1140 West Adams Boulevard

HCM #330
Rosedale Cemetery
1831 West Washington
Boulevard

HCM #466
Henry J. Foster Residence
1030 West 23rd Street

HCM #200
Second Baptist Church Building
2412 Griffith Avenue

295

200

330

466

606

HCM #606
Kerkhoff House
734 West Adams Boulevard

HCM #409
Burkhalter Residence
2309-2311 Scarff Street

HCM #467
Chalet Apartments
2375 Scarff Street

HCM #678
Furlong House
2657 South Van Buren Place

678

409

467

2375

197

HCM #197
Britt Mansion and Formal Gardens
2141 West Adams Boulevard

HCM #609
Powers Apartments #3
2310 Scarff Street

HCM #608
Powers Apartments #2
2326 Scarff Street

609

608

83

500

70

297

HCM #229
Westminster Presbyterian Church
2230 West Jefferson Boulevard

HCM #626
Eyraud Residence
1326 South Manhattan Place

HCM #407
Seyler Residence
2305 Scarff Street

229

407

HCM #258
Fitzgerald House
3115 West Adams Boulevard

HCM #507
Hiram V. Short Residence
2110 Estrella Avenue

HCM #621
Alice Lynch Residence
2414 4th Avenue

258

507

621

561

HCM #561
Allen House
2125 Bonsallo Avenue

HCM #496
Lycurgus Lindsay Mansion
3424 West Adams Boulevard

HCM #478
Guasti Villa/
Busby Berkeley Estate
3500 West Adams Boulevard

HCM #417
Gordon L. McDonough House
2532 5th Avenue

417

496

478

610

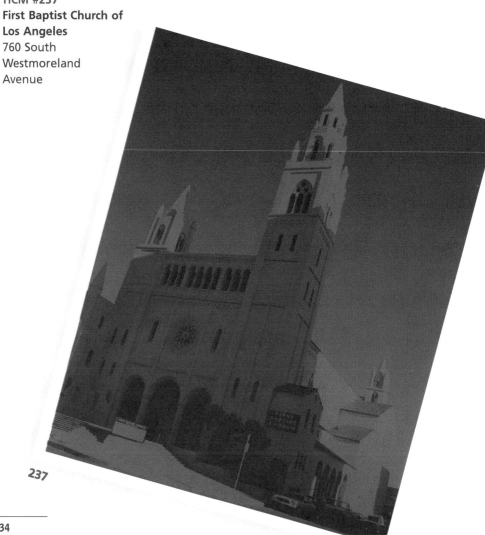

HCM #610
Shankland House
715 West 28th Street

HCM #244
Residence
1866 West 14th Street

HCM #660
Rosenheim Mansion
1120 South Westchester
Place

HCM #237
**First Baptist Church of
Los Angeles**
760 South
Westmoreland
Avenue

237

660

516

HCM #516
St. John's Episcopal Church
514 West Adams Boulevard

HCM #212
Stimson Residence
2421 South Figueroa Street

HCM #456
Ezra T. Stimson House
839 West Adams Boulevard

HCM #169
Residence of
William Grant Still
1262 Victoria Avenuea

169

456

103

497

434

654

HCM #242
Miller & Herriott Tract House
1163 West 27th Street

HCM #551
Thomas W. Phillips Residence
2215 South Harvard Boulevard

HCM #578
Emanuel Danish Evangelical Lutheran Church
4254-4260 3rd Avenue

242

551

578

86

HCM #86
Powers Residence
1345 Alvarado Terrace

HCM #296
John C. Harrison House
1160 West 27th Street

HCM #241
Sunshine Mission
2600 South Hoover Street

HCM #602
Auguste Marquis Residence/
Filipino Federation of America
2302 West 25th Street

602

519

HCM #519
Cockins House
2653 South Hoover Street

HCM #601
Gramercy Park Homestead
2102 West 24th Street

HCM #341
**First African Methodist
Episcopal Zion Cathedral
and Community Center**
1449 West Adams
Boulevard

HCM #335
Henry J. Reuman Residence
925 West 23rd Street

335

601

341

477

Briggs Residence
3734 West Adams Boulevard

Durfee House
1007 West 24th Street

(Site of) Residence
919 West 20th Street

**Margaret T. and
Bettie Mead Creighton
Residence**
2342 Scarff Street

455

273

179

HCM #458
Wells-Halliday Mansion
2146 West Adams Boulevard

HCM #531
Wilshire Ward Chapel
1209 South Manhattan Place

HCM #583
Zobelein Estate
3738-3770 South Flower Street

531

583

599

The western edge of Los Angeles was developed primarily in the 1920s. This sector has planned communities such as Westwood, modeled on Mediterranean villages, and park-like, residential Brentwood. In Westwood, the Spanish Classical Revival Fox Village Theatre (HCM #362) typifies the architectural style used as the visual theme of the village, while the Janss Investment Company Building (HCM #364) housed the Westwood developer's offices beneath its distinctive dome. The Courtyard Apartment Complex (HCM #447) was constructed in 1935 and its Monterey style, a variation on Spanish Colonial Revival, continues the architectural theme that dominates Westwood. In nearby Brentwood, the 1939 Gas Station (HCM #387) has a two-story central tower typical of the service stations that once existed in Westwood. Southeast of Westwood is the Moreton Bay Fig Tree (HCM #19) at National Boulevard and Military Avenue. Planted in 1875, it is a magnificent specimen, a prerequisite for trees that are designated as Historic-Cultural Monuments. Farther west, in Pacific Palisades, is the Case Study House #8, Eames House, Studio and Grounds (HCM #381). Designed by Charles Eames between 1947 and 1949, it is one of several steel-and-glass structures that employ spare, industrial design in residential architecture.

325

254

319

231

HCM #38
(Site of) Founder's Oak
Haverford Avenue
between Sunset Boulevard
and Antioch Street

HCM #365
Kelton Apartments
644 Kelton Avenue

HCM #279
Greenacres
1040 Angelo Drive

HCM #435
**Andalusia Apartments
and Gardens**
1471-1475 Havenhurst Drive

38

435

365

279

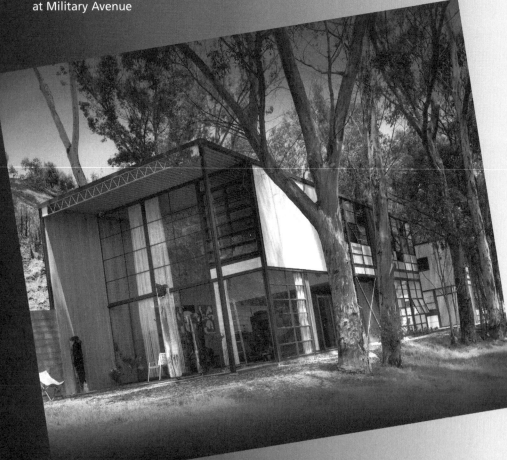

381

13

HCM #13
Rocha House
2400 Shenandoah
Street

HCM #647
Sten/Frenke-Gould
Residence
126 Mabery Road

HCM #368
Elkay Apartments
638 Kelton Avenue

HCM #530
John Entenza House
(Case Study House #9)
205 Chautauqua Boulevard

530

647

368

669

HCM #669
**Bailey House
(Case Study House #21)**
9038 Wonderland Park Avenue

HCM #670
**Stahl House
(Case Study House #22)**
1635 Woods Drive

HCM #547
Camp Josepho, Malibu Lodge
3000 Rustic Canyon Road

HCM #148
Coral Trees
Median strip of San Vicente
Boulevard between 26th Street
and Bringham Avenue

148

670

547

HCM #681
Schott House
907 Hanley Avenue

HCM #637
Campbell Divertimento
Fountain
1150 Brooklawn Drive

HCM #635
Weckler House
12434 Rochedale Lane

HCM #506
Tischler Residence
175 Greenfield
Avenue

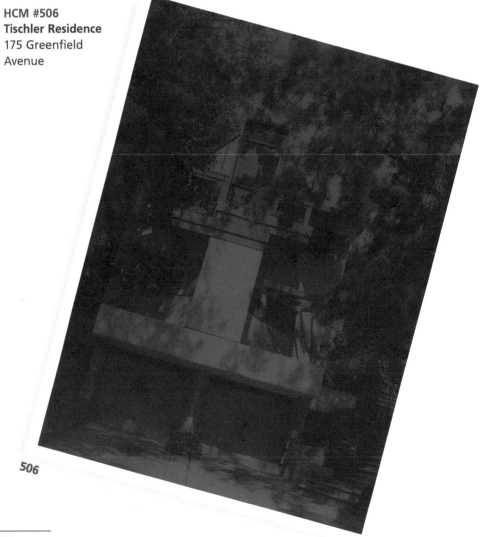

506

635

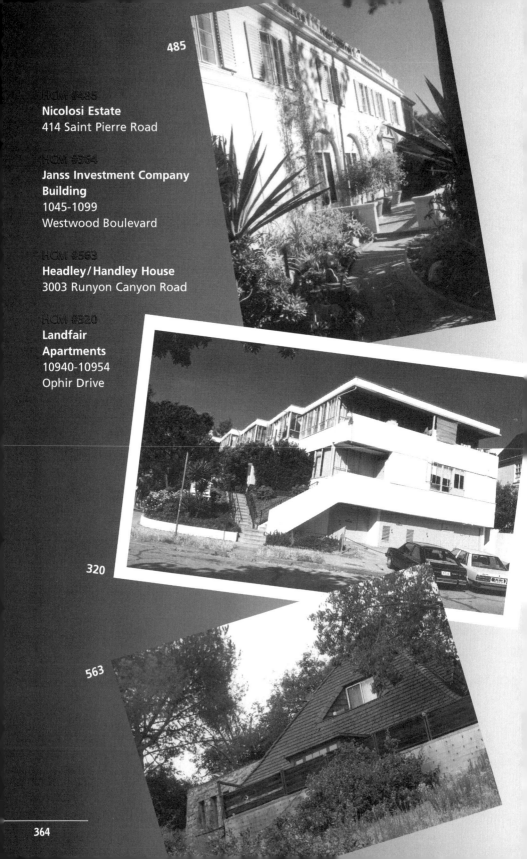

485

HCM #485
Nicolosi Estate
414 Saint Pierre Road

HCM #364
Janss Investment Company Building
1045-1099
Westwood Boulevard

HCM #563
Headley/Handley House
3003 Runyon Canyon Road

HCM #320
Landfair Apartments
10940-10954
Ophir Drive

320

563

364

697

HCM #697
Kermin House
900 Stonehill Lane

HCM #465
Sycamore Trees
Located on Bienveneda Avenue
(South from Sunset Boulevard
to the cul-de-sac)

HCM #633
Haas House
12404 Rochedale Lane

HCM #623
Kappe Residence
715 Brooktree Road

623

465

633

668

HCM #668
Hillside House
8707 St. Ives Drive

HCM #634
Kalmick House
12327 Rochedale Lane

HCM #446
**Courtyard Apartment
Complex**
10830 Lindbrook Drive

634

446

233

HCM #233
(Site of) Sunset Plaza
Apartments
1220 Sunset Plaza Drive

HCM #360
Bratskeller/Egyptian Theatre
1142-1154
Westwood Boulevard

HCM #682
S. H. Woodruff Residence
3185 Durand Drive

HCM #351
Strathmore Apartments
11005-11013½
Strathmore Drive

351

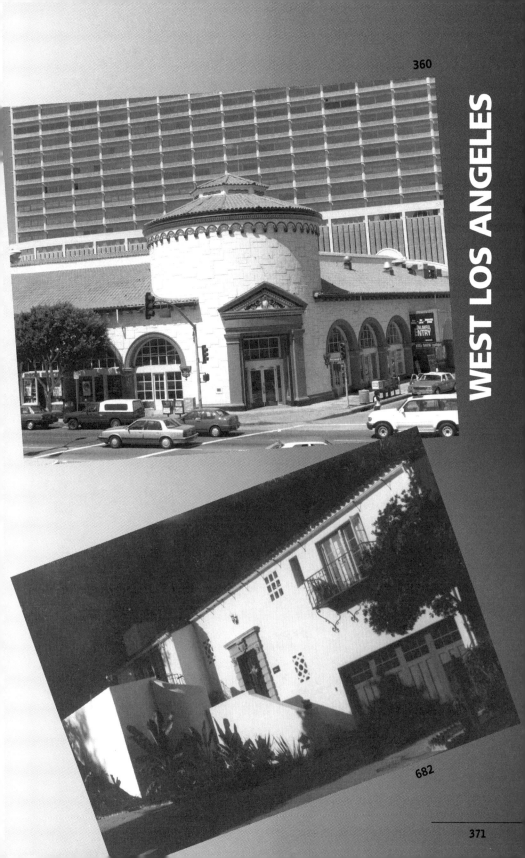

682

324

655

440

WEST LOS ANGELES

594

HCM #694
Emmons House
661 Brooktree Lane

HCM #636
C. A. Fellows Residence
1215 Westchester Place

HCM #490
Sa-Angna
4231-4363 South Lincoln
Boulevard and Admiralty Way

HCM #632
Goldenfeld House
810 Bramble Way

694

632

636

490

HCM #387
Gas Station
110 South Barrington Avenue

HCM #318
Holmby House
1221-1223 Holmby Avenue

HCM #577
Sturges House
441-449 Skyewiay Road

HCM #693
Israel House
914 Bluegrass Lane

387

318

577

693

663

HCM #663
Uplifters Clubhouse
601 Latimer Road

HCM #362
Fox Village Theatre
945 Broxton Avenue

HCM #367
Sheets Apartments
10901-10919
Strathmore Drive

HCM #589
**Feuchtwanger
House**
520 Paseo
Miramar

589

367

182

HCM #182
Ivy Substation
9015 Venice Boulevard

HCM #698
Sherwood House
947 Stonehill Lane

HCM #696
Jones and Emmons
Building
12248 Santa Monica
Boulevard

HCM #276
Pacific Palisades
Business Block
15300-15318 Sunset Boulevard

276

S.M.L. & W. Co. Collection

695

HCM #695
Gross House
860 Hanley Avenue

HCM #361
Fox Bruin Theater
926-940 Broxton Avenue

HCM #363
Gayley Terrace
959 Gayley Avenue

361

363

HCM #680
**Mutual Housing
Association Site Office**
990 Hanley Avenue

HCM #685
**Pascual Marquez
Family Cemetery**
635 San Lorenzo Street

680

685

Just west of downtown is Westlake, which was developed in the late nineteenth century. Its centerpiece is General Douglas MacArthur Park (HCM #100). Named Westlake Park in 1890, when the existing pond was enlarged, it was renamed in 1942 at the height of the military leader's popularity. Overlooking the lake is the twelve-story Beaux Arts Park Plaza Hotel (HCM #267), completed for the Elk's Club in 1925. Nearby is the 1929 Art Deco Chouinard Institute of the Arts (HCM #454). With Otis Art Institute and Art Center School of Design also in the neighborhood at the time, the locale housed the city's three major art schools. Representative of the eclectic residential design of an earlier period is the Victorian Residence (HCM #45) built in 1894. Built in 1929 for the carriage trade is the Bullock's Wilshire Building (HCM #56), home to the legendary department store. Clad in buff terra cotta, copper and glass, this Art Deco landmark features an exceptional tower and grand porte-cochère. To the west is Hancock Park, a venerable residential neighborhood that includes the strip of commercial buildings lining Wilshire Boulevard. The Los Altos Apartments (HCM #311) were built in 1925 and are an elegant example of Spanish Revival architecture. Film stars Bette Davis, Clara Bow and Charlie Chaplin kept apartments there, as did William Randolph Hearst. The Higgins/Verbeck/Hirsch Mansion (HCM #403) is typical of the grand houses that once lined Wilshire Boulevard. This 1902 residence was relocated from Wilshire to Lucerne Boulevard in 1924 to make way for commercial development. Just north of Hancock Park on Beverly Boulevard, the notable Einar C. Petersen Studio Court (HCM #552) was built in 1921. Consructed by its namesake, an artist responsible for numerous murals in downtown, the Storybook-style structures resemble a street in the town of Abeltoft, Denmark, where Petersen was born.

91

HCM #91
Korean Philadelphia
Presbyterian Church
407 South New Hampshire

HCM #39
Residence
1425 Miramar Street

HCM #100
General Douglas MacArthur Park
2230 West 6th Street

WESTLAKE–HANCOCK PARK

309

311

239

333

326

HCM #326
(Site of)
The McKinley Mansion
310 South Lafayette Park Place

HCM #646
Villa Serrano
930-940 South Serrano Avenue

HCM #116
Wilshire Boulevard Temple
3663 Wilshire Boulevard

HCM #641
**Brynmoor Apartments
Neon Roof Sign**
432-436 South
New Hampshire Avenue

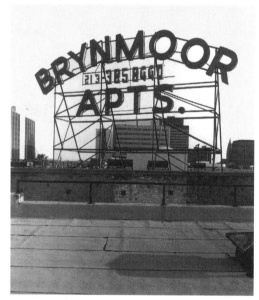

641

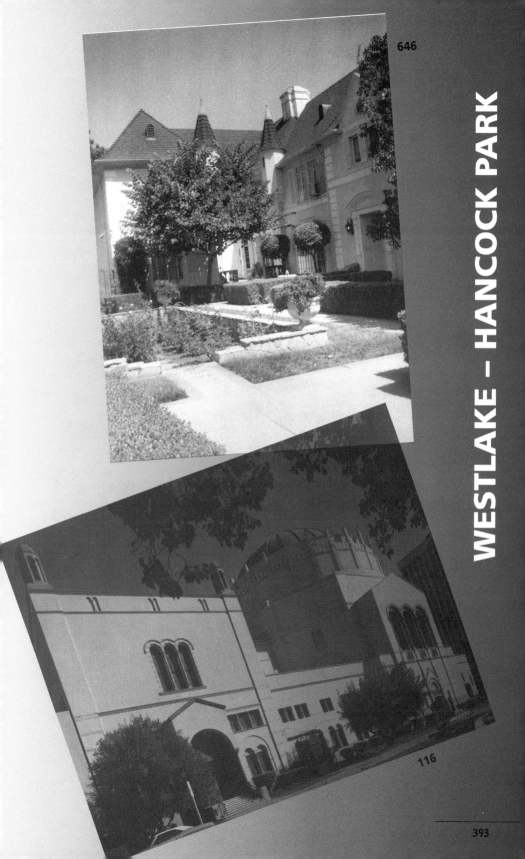

646

116

643

HCM #643
**Superba Apartments
Incandescent Roof Sign**
335 South Berendo
Street

HCM #432
Doria Apartments
1600 West Pico
Boulevard

HCM #268
**La Fonda Restaurant
Building**
2501 Wilshire Boulevard

HCM #649
**Cora B. Henderson
House**
132 South Wilton Place

649

432

268

HCM #56
Bullock's Wilshire Building
3050 Wilshire Boulevard

HCM #619
Wolff-Fifield House
111 North June Street

HCM #115
Evans
Residence
419 South
Lorraine
Boulevard

56

WESTLAKE – HANCOCK PARK

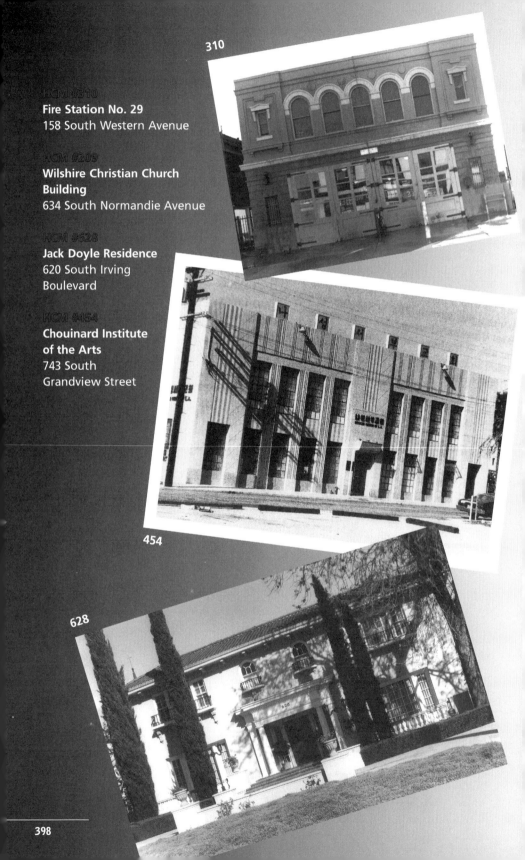

310

454

628

209

491

HCM #491
**Charles B. Booth Residence
and Carriage House**
824 South Bonnie Brae Street

HCM #642
**Embassy Apartments
Neon Roof Sign**
702-708
South Mariposa Avenue

HCM #415
Wilshire Branch Library
149 North St. Andrews Place

642

415

568

HCM #568
Thomas A. Churchill, Sr.
Residence
215 South Wilton Place

HCM #167
Residence
826 South Coronado

HCM #250
Ebell of Los Angeles
4400 Wilshire Boulevard

HCM #684
Heart House
112 North Harvard
Boulevard

684

WESTLAKE – HANCOCK PARK

250

650

HCM #650
Mortensen House
103 South Wilton Drive

HCM #618
McDonnell Residence
Founder's Home: Urban Academy
601 North Wilcox Avenue

HCM #534
I. Magnin & Co. Building
3240 Wilshire Boulevard

HCM #114
Wilshire United Methodist Church
4350 Wilshire Boulevard

114

618

534

158

Archives of the Society of Mt. Carmel

214

546

576

HCM #267
Park Plaza Hotel
607 South Park View Street

HCM #639
Ruskin Art Club
800 South Plymouth Boulevard

HCM #129
Residence
767 Garland Avenue

267

129

403

HCM #403
Higgins/Verbeck/Hirsch Mansion
637 South Lucerne Boulevard

HCM #538
David J. Witmer Family
Houses and Compound
208, 210, 210½ Witmer Street
and 1422 West 2nd Street

HCM #238
Granada Buildings
672 South Lafayette
Park Place

HCM #552
Einar C. Petersen Studio Court
4350-4352¾
Beverly Boulevard

552

538

GRANADA
BUILDINGS

238

280

653

328

HCM #431
Residence
1851 West 11th Street

HCM #555
Mother Trust Superet Center
2512-2516 West 3rd Street

HCM #327
Thomas Potter Residence
1135 South Alvarado Street

431

555

327

433

Historic-Cultural Monument designation is awarded to sites, structures and other landmarks that are, in one way or another, important markers in the history of Los Angeles. In the instance of two particular monument designations, the impact has been significant even though they are located outside the city's limits. The bronze plaque at Manzanar (HCM #160) details the effect this site had on the citizens of Los Angeles during World War II: "Manzanar was declared a Historic-Cultural Monument to remind us that the site was used as a war relocation center, unjustly confining 10,000 persons of Japanese ancestry, many of whom were American citizens, from March 1942 to December 1945. Seventy percent of the Los Angeles Japanese American community were sent to Manzanar during the war. It was the first of the ten such camps that would eventually be used to intern 110,000 people. The site was bounded by barbed wire and guard towers." The only other city-designated monument that lies outside the city's bounds is the S.S. Catalina (HCM #213). The "Great White Steamship," as S.S. Catalina was known to Angelenos, was christened on May 24, 1924, and began ferrying passengers between San Pedro and the resort of Santa Catalina Island. Its capacity was 1,950 passengers. On December 6, 1941, when Santa Catalina became a military training area, the S.S. Catalina was requisitioned by the War Department. During World War II, it carried a total of 820,199 soldiers, more than any other Army transport. In 1946, the ship resumed regular service, which continued until 1972. In 1983, the S.S. Catalina was towed to Ensenada, Mexico, where its next assignment is uncertain.

HCM #213
S.S. *Catalina*
("The Great White Steamship")
Port of Ensenada

HCM #160
Manzanar
Inyo County on Highway 395

213

160

PART 2

HCM #1
LEONIS ADOBE
23537 Calabasas Road, Calabasas. Built in the Monterey style in the 1840s, it was occupied by Miguel Leonis, one of the most colorful and influential figures of early Los Angeles in the 1870s. Open to the public.
Declared: 8/6/1962 *(pg. 237)*

HCM #2
BOLTON HALL
10116 Commerce Avenue, Tujunga. Built in 1913 by master mason George Harris for use as a community center, Bolton Hall is constructed of native stone.
Declared: 8/6/1962 *(pg. 251)*

HCM #3
PLAZA CHURCH
100 West Sunset Boulevard, Los Angeles. Built in 1822 and designed by Jose Antonio Ramirez, it is recognized as the oldest established church in continuing use in Los Angeles.
Declared: 8/6/1962 *(pg. 26)*

HCM #4
ANGEL'S FLIGHT
4th and Hill Streets, Los Angeles (original location at 3rd and Hill Streets). Built in 1901 and designed by J.W. Eddy, it was often called the "world's shortest railway." Until it was dismantled and put in storage in 1969, it served an essential function of transportation to Bunker Hill. In 1992 a new location was chosen, and in February 1996 Angel's Flight was reopened at 4th and Hill Streets following a careful reconstruction incorporating the original station buildings and the original cars, known as "Olivet" and "Sinai." On February 1, 2001 a cable unraveled and the upper car collided with the lower one, closing the railway once again.
Declared: 8/6/1962 *(pg. 27)*

HCM #5
THE SALT BOX
(Destroyed) (original location at 339 South Bunker Hill Avenue). Built in 1880, it was destroyed by fire after relocation to Heritage Square (3800 Homer Street, Los Angeles) in 1969.
Declared: 8/6/1962 *(pg. 27)*

HCM #6
BRADBURY BUILDING
304 South Broadway, Los Angeles. Built in 1893, this unique, five-story office building by George H. Wyman is notable for its interior court with skylight and open corridors, open-cage elevators and ornamental rails and stairs.
Declared: 9/21/1962 *(pg. 68)*

HCM #7
ANDRES PICO ADOBE
10940 Sepulveda Boulevard, Mission Hills. This 1834 adobe is plastered and set on a fieldstone foundation. Open to the public.
Declared: 9/21/1962 *(pg. 239)*

HCM #8
FOY HOUSE
1337-1341 Carroll Avenue, Los Angeles (original location at the intersection of 7th and Figueroa Streets; relocated to 633 South Witmer Street 1919-1921). The residence of Mary E. Foy, the first woman to hold the office of City Librarian in 1880, the residence was moved to its present location in 1993.
Declared: 9/21/1962 *(pg. 82)*

HCM #9
SHADOW RANCH
22633 Vanowen Street, Canoga Park. Constructed between 1869 and 1872 on the original Workman Ranch, this house is adobe and redwood.
Declared:11/2/1962 *(pg. 252)*

HCM #10
EAGLE ROCK
Northern terminus of Figueroa Street, Eagle Rock. Noted by Spanish explorers, its distinguishing feature is the figure of an eagle in flight, a natural formation. Declared:11/16/1962 *(pg. 161)*

HCM #11
(Site of) THE ROCHESTER
1012 West Temple Street, Los Angeles. This wood frame building was then one of the very few examples of the Second Empire (Napoleon III) style in Los Angeles. Prior to being dismantled on February 14, 1979, the building had been at the temporary site of Alameda Street and San Bruno since September 30, 1970.
Declared: 1/4/1963 *(pg. 68)*

HCM #12
HOLLYHOCK HOUSE
Barnsdall Art Park, 4808 Hollyhock Boulevard, Los Angeles. This was the first residence designed by architect Frank Lloyd Wright in the Los Angeles region. Open to the public.
Declared: 1/4/1963 *(pg. 119)*

HCM #13
ROCHA HOUSE
2400 Shenandoah Street, Los Angeles. The residence was built in 1865 by Antonio Jose Rocha II on a large portion of *Rancho Rincon de los Bueyes.*
Declared: 1/28/1963 *(pg. 358)*

HCM #14
CHATSWORTH COMMUNITY CHURCH
Oakwood Memorial Park, 22601 Lassen Street, Chatsworth (original location at 10051 Topanga Canyon Boulevard). Built in 1903, it is the oldest public building in Chatsworth.
Declared: 2/15/1963 *(pg. 238)*

HCM #15
TOWERS OF SIMON RODIA (WATTS TOWERS)
1765 East 107th Street, Watts. Built between 1921 and 1954, the internationally acclaimed Watts Towers (as they are known colloquially) were constructed by Italian immigrant Simon Rodia. Open to the public.
Declared: 3/1/1963 *(pg. 260)*

HCM #16
(Site of) ST. JOSEPH'S CHURCH
218 East 12th Street, Los Angeles. Built in 1901, this Victorian Gothic structure's originally plain interiors were elaborately stenciled in 1928. It was destroyed by fire September 4, 1983.
Declared: 5/10/1963 *(pg. 69)*

HCM #17
ST. VIBIANA'S CATHEDRAL
114 East 2nd Street, Los Angeles. Designed by architects Ezra F. Kysor and W.J. Mathews, it was dedicated on April 30, 1876. John C. Austin designed extensive renovations that were completed in 1922.
Declared: 5/10/1963 *(pg. 69)*

HCM #18
(Site of) HYDE PARK CONGREGATIONAL CHURCH
6501 Crenshaw Boulevard, Los Angeles. This tiny wood church was characterized by two front-corner towers, one of which contained a belfry. It was also known for its stained glass windows (demolished 1964).
Declared: 5/10/1963. *(pg. 16)*

HCM #19
MORETON BAY FIG TREE
11000 National Boulevard at Military Avenue, Los Angeles. Planted in 1875, *Ficus Macrophylla* is described as the greatest of Australian avenue trees.
Declared: 5/10/1963 *(pg. 357)*

HCM #20
TWO STONE GATES
Intersection of Beachwood, Westshire and Belden Drives, Hollywood Hills. Built by European stonemasons in the early 1920s, the gates are the official entrance to the community of Hollywoodland.
Declared: 5/24/1963 *(pg. 118)*

HCM #21
DRUM BARRACKS AND OFFICERS' QUARTERS
1052 Banning Boulevard, Wilmington. This Italianate building is one of two surviving 1862 structures that comprised Camp Drum, the United States Army headquarters for California, Arizona and New Mexico during the Civil War. Camp Drum, named in honor of General Richard Coulter Drum, Commander of the Army's Department of the Far West, was a sixty-acre military garrison constructed in Wilmington to protect the West from becoming a Confederate stronghold. Open to the public.
Declared: 6/7/1963 *(pg. 261)*

HCM #22
THE PALMS-SOUTHERN PACIFIC RAILROAD DEPOT
Heritage Square, 3800 Homer Street, Los Angeles (original location at National Boulevard and Vinton Avenue). This circa 1886 railroad depot was relocated in 1976.
Declared: 8/9/1963 *(pg. 160)*

HCM #23
SAN FERNANDO MISSION
15151 San Fernando Mission Boulevard, Mission Hills. The present church is a reconstructed version of the original 1797 mission, which was demolished after the 1971 San Fernando Valley earthquake. The original convent building still remains on the site. It was seventeenth in the chain of missions.
Declared: 8/9/1963 *(pg. 246)*

HCM #24
(Site of) OAK TREE
Louise Avenue, 210 feet south of Ventura Boulevard, Encino. The tree, *Quercus Agrifolia,* was judged to be over 1,000 years old. It was destroyed by storms in January 1997.
Declared: 9/6/1963 *(pg. 241)*

HCM #25
GENERAL PHINEAS BANNING RESIDENCE AND BANNING PARK
Banning Park, 401 East M Street, Wilmington. Built in 1864, it was the home of General Phineas Banning, founder of Wilmington, California in 1858. Open to the public.
Declared:10/11/1963 (residence); 12/18/2001(park) *(pg. 263)*

HCM #26
(Site of) THE FIRST CEMETERY IN THE CITY OF LOS ANGELES
521 North Main Street, Los Angeles. Built from 1823 to 1844, it was the first grave-yard adjacent to the Plaza Church. It is believed to contain buried remains of the Christian indigenous inhabitants of Yang-Na, a Gabrieleño village, and the early Spanish and Mexican settlers.
Declared: 3/20/1964 *(pg. 71)*

HCM #27
THE CASTLE
(Destroyed) (original location at 325 South Bunker Hill Avenue, Los Angeles). Built circa 1882, it contained many fine examples of late nineteenth-century crafts-manship. In 1969 it was moved to Heritage Square (3800 Homer Street, Los Angeles) and, while awaiting restoration, was burned to the ground by vandals.
Declared: 5/8/1964 *(pg. 70)*

HCM #28
WILLIAM ANDREWS CLARK MEMORIAL LIBRARY
2520 Cimarron Street, Los Angeles. Completed in 1926, this Renaissance Revival building was designed by Robert D. Farquhar. Open to the public.
Declared:10/9/1964 *(pg. 294)*

HCM #29
CAMPO DE CAHUENGA
3919 Lankershim Boulevard, North Hollywood. Site of the signing of the Treaty of Cahuenga on January 13, 1847. Open to the public.
Declared:11/13/1964 *(pg. 244)*

HCM #30
DOHENY MANSION
8 Chester Place, Los Angeles. Built in 1899 and designed by Eisen & Hunt, it is one of the best-preserved and most impressive late-Victorian mansions remaining in the West Adams district.
Declared: 1/8/1965 *(pg. 305)*

HCM #31
ORCUTT RANCH HORTICULTURE CENTER (*RANCHO SOMBRA DEL ROBLE*)
23555 Justice Street, Canoga Park. This 1920 adobe residence was the home of W.W. Orcutt, the Union Oil geologist whose 1901 discovery of prehistoric fossils in the La Brea Tar Pits led to massive excavations there. Open to the public.
Declared: 1/22/1965 *(pg. 237)*

HCM #32
ST. SAVIOUR'S CHAPEL
Harvard School, 3700 Coldwater Canyon Avenue, Studio City. Designer Reginald Johnson patterned this chapel, with the pews facing the center aisle, after the Chapel at Rugby School in England. It was dedicated in 1914.
Declared: 2/5/1965 *(pg. 240)*

HCM #33
RESIDENCE "A"
Barnsdall Art Park, 4800 Hollywood Boulevard, Los Angeles. Designed by Frank Lloyd Wright, it was built in 1919 for Aline Barnsdall as part of a proposed cultural center for performing arts.
Declared: 2/26/1965 *(pg. 120)*

HCM #34
BARNSDALL ART PARK
4800 Hollywood Boulevard, Los Angeles. Eleven acres on the crown of Olive Hill were donated to the City of Los Angeles in 1927 by Aline Barnsdall with the stipulation that the land be used for a park and playground. It is the site of the Los Angeles Municipal Art Gallery, Junior Arts Center, Hollyhock House, Gallery Theater and Barnsdall Arts Center.
Declared: 2/26/1965 *(pg. 118)*

HCM #35
BIRTHPLACE OF ADLAI E. STEVENSON
2639 Monmouth Avenue, Los Angeles. Adlai E. Stevenson, an internationally known political figure, was born in this house on February 5, 1900. At the time of his death in 1965, he was the United States Ambassador to the United Nations.
Declared: 8/20/1965 *(pg. 292)*

HCM #36
WATTS STATION
1686 East 103rd Street, Watts. The station is representative of wood frame construction used in the new towns clustering around Los Angeles in the early 1900s.
Declared:12/3/1965 *(pg. 263)*

HCM #37
FIRE STATION No. 23
225 East 5th Street, Los Angeles. Commissioned in 1910 at a cost of $57,000, it is unique in its construction and advanced in the design of its living and working quarters.
Declared: 2/18/1966 *(pg. 70)*

HCM #38
(Site of) FOUNDER'S OAK
Haverford Avenue between Sunset Boulevard and Antioch Street, Pacific Palisades. Quercus agrifolia (Coast Live Oak) played a significant role in the establishment of Pacific Palisades. In August 1975 the tree had to be cut down due to termite infestation.
Declared: 3/25/1966 *(pg. 354)*

HCM #39
RESIDENCE
1425 Miramar Street, Los Angeles. Built circa 1890, it was designed by architect Joseph Cather Newsom.
Declared: 6/15/1966 *(pg. 387)*

HCM #40
HALE HOUSE
Heritage Square, 3800 Homer Street, Los Angeles (original location at 4425 North Figueroa Street). This 1886 Queen Anne and Eastlake style residence was designed by W.R. Norton and moved to Heritage Square in 1970.
Declared: 6/15/1966 *(pg. 161)*

HCM #41
144 DEODAR TREES
White Oak Avenue between San Fernando Mission Boulevard and San Jose Street, Granada Hills. These *Cedrus Deodara* trees were planted in 1932. They are native to the Himalayas and valued for their size, beauty and timber.
Declared: 8/3/1966 *(pg. 247)*

HCM #42
SAN ANTONIO WINERY
737 Lamar Street, Lincoln Heights. Founded in 1917, it is the last remaining winery in the City of Los Angeles.
Declared: 9/14/1966 *(pg. 71)*

HCM #43
CALIFORNIA CLUB BUILDING
538 South Flower Street, Los Angeles. Designed by architect Robert D. Farquhar and completed in 1930, this Beaux Arts building is clad with Roman face-bricks and granite and tufa stone trim.
Declared:11/2/1966 *(pg. 72)*

HCM #44
HANGAR No. 1 BUILDING
5701 West Imperial Highway, Los Angeles. Constructed in 1929, Hangar No. 1 was the first structure built at Mines Field, now Los Angeles International Airport.
Declared:11/16/1966 *(pg. 17)*

HCM #45
RESIDENCE
818 South Bonnie Brae Street, Los Angeles. Considered a prototype of distinctive architecture of the 1880s boom in Los Angeles, it is representative of the eclecticism in building design between 1870 and 1900.
Declared: 2/8/1967 *(pg. 390)*

HCM #46
CENTRAL LIBRARY BUILDING
630 West 5th Street, Los Angeles. Dedicated on July 15, 1926, this distinctive landmark was the last major work of Bertram Grosvenor Goodhue. After a devastating 1986 arson fire, the building was completely restored.
Declared: 3/1/1967 *(pg. 72)*

HCM #47
ST. JOHN'S EPISCOPAL CHURCH
1537 Neptune Avenue, Wilmington (original location at 422 Canal Street, now Avalon Boulevard). Built in 1883, the church was moved from its original location to its present site in 1943. It is the oldest church building in the harbor area that is still used for regular worship services.
Declared: 3/15/1967 *(pg. 262)*

HCM #48
CHAVEZ RAVINE ARBORETUM
Elysian Park, Los Angeles. This area was Southern California's first botanical garden. In 1893 the Los Angeles Horticultural Society began planting of rare trees in the upper part of the ravine.
Declared: 4/26/1967 *(pg. 85)*

HCM #49
76 MATURE OLIVE TREES
Lining both sides of Lassen Street between Topanga Canyon Boulevard and Farralone Avenue, Chatsworth. Native to the eastern Mediterranean region, olive trees were introduced to California by Franciscan missionaries. These particular trees approximate the age of Chatsworth itself, having been planted in the latter part of the 19th century.
Declared: 5/10/1967 *(pg. 243)*

HCM #50
MISSION WELLS AND THE SETTLING BASIN
Havana and Bleeker Streets, Sylmar. The presence of cienegas or swamp lands was one of the vital factors in the decision of the Franciscan Padres to erect the Mission San Fernando *Rey de España* in 1797 at a site two to three miles west of these cienegas.
Declared: 5/10/1967 *(pg. 240)*

HCM #51
RESIDENCE
1300 Carroll Avenue, Los Angeles. Built by Aaron P. Phillips circa 1880, it is an ornate example of both the Queen Anne and Eastlake styles.
Declared: 5/10/1967 *(pg. 82)*

HCM #52
RESIDENCE
1330 Carroll Avenue, Los Angeles. Built circa 1880, this twelve-room house was constructed for dairyman Charles Sessions by architect Joseph Cather Newsom.
Declared: 5/24/1967 *(pg. 84)*

HCM #53
ST. PETER'S EPISCOPAL CHURCH
Harbor View Memorial Park, 2330 South Grand Avenue, San Pedro (original location on Beacon Street between 2nd and 3rd Streets). The first service in this church was held on Easter Sunday, April 13, 1884. In September 1956, a three-year campaign to save San Pedro's oldest church was successful.
Declared:12/6/1967 *(pg. 261)*

HCM #54
(Site of) OLD SIXTH STREET WOODEN BRIDGE
Hollenbeck Park Lake, Los Angeles. Built in 1898, the bridge was a picturesque feature. It was declared unsafe and dismantled in 1968.
Declared: 5/22/1968 *(pg. 105)*

HCM #55
GRAUMAN'S CHINESE THEATRE (MANN'S CHINESE THEATRE)
6925 Hollywood Boulevard, Hollywood. Sid Grauman's second theater in Hollywood opened on May 18, 1927 with Cecil B. DeMille's film *The King of Kings.* Designed by Meyer & Holler and Oriental in its colorful décor, it is also noted for the forecourt, where movie star hand prints and footprints are impressed in cement.
Declared: 6/5/1968 *(pg. 121)*

HCM #56
BULLOCK'S WILSHIRE BUILDING
3050 Wilshire Boulevard, Los Angeles. Built in 1929 and designed by John and Donald Parkinson, the building has been termed the American version of Parisian Moderne. The design makes striking use of buff terra cotta, copper and glass.
Declared: 6/5/1968 *(pg. 396)*

HCM #57
SECOND CHURCH OF CHRIST, SCIENTIST OF LOS ANGELES
948 West Adams Boulevard, Los Angeles. Construction started in March 1907 and was completed in January 1910 at a cost of $318,500. Designed by architect Alfred F. Rosenheim, the building is an example of Beaux Arts Classicism with Italian-Renaissance influence.
Declared: 7/17/1968 *(pg. 296)*

HCM #58
A & M RECORDS STUDIO (formerly the Charlie Chaplin Studio)
1416 North La Brea Avenue, Hollywood. Built in 1919, it was one of the first complete motion picture studios in Hollywood.
Declared: 2/5/69 *(pg. 120)*

HCM #59
EAGLE ROCK CITY HALL
2035 Colorado Boulevard, Eagle Rock. This tri-level, Spanish tile-roofed building was constructed in 1922, eleven years after Eagle Rock was incorporated as a city. In 1923 Eagle Rock became a part of the City of Los Angeles and the building became the first city hall to be acquired by Los Angeles through the process of annexation.
Declared: 2/26/1969 *(pg. 162)*

HCM #60
BILTMORE HOTEL
515 South Olive Street, Los Angeles. Designed by Schultze & Weaver in 1922, it is located on land that was once a part of the original four-square leagues owned by *El Pueblo de Nuestra Señora la Reina Los Angeles.*
Declared: 7/2/1969 *(pg. 73)*

HCM #61
(Site of) PHILHARMONIC AUDITORIUM
427 West 5th Street, Los Angeles. Once the largest concrete-reinforced building in Los Angeles, it was also the first theater to have a balcony without supporting pillars. The grand opening of the auditorium took place November 8, 1906 (demolished 1984).
Declared: 7/2/1969 *(pg. 73)*

HCM #62
JUDSON STUDIOS
200 South Avenue 66, Garvanza. Founded in 1897 by master craftsmen working in stained glass and mosaics, the original building was designed in 1900 by William Lees Judson. It was rebuilt after a fire in 1909 from a design by Train & Williams.
Declared: 8/13/1969 *(pg. 163)*

HCM #63
McGROARTY HOME
7570 McGroarty Terrace,
Tujunga. John Steven
McGroarty was Poet
Laureate of the State of
California from 1933 until
his death in 1944. Built in
1923, his residence and
approximately sixteen acres
of land have since been
acquired by the City of Los
Angeles. This fieldstone and
stucco home designed by
Arthur B. Benton is now
used for art classes.
Declared: 2/4/1970 *(pg. 246)*

HCM #64
PLAZA PARK
Area approximately bound-
ed by Cesar E. Chavez
Avenue, Alameda, Los
Angeles, Arcadia, New High
and Main Streets, Los
Angeles. Part of the original
Spanish land grant, it was
on the plaza that Governor
Felipe de Neve conducted
formal ceremonies on
September 4, 1781 establish-
ing *El Pueblo de Nuestra*
Señora la Reina de Los
Angeles. The present site of
the existing plaza is not pre-
cisely its original location.
Declared: 4/1/1970 *(pg. 80)*

HCM #65
VALLEY KNUDSEN GARDEN
RESIDENCE
Heritage Square, 3800
Homer Street, Los Angeles
(original location on
Johnston Street). Experts
date the building as circa
1880 and describe it as "a
19th-century Mansard-style
residence . . . one of the last
examples of its style in the
Los Angeles area." It was
relocated in 1971.
Declared: 4/15/1970 *(pg. 162)*

HCM #66
(Site of) ST. PAUL'S
CATHEDRAL
615 South Figueroa Street,
Los Angeles. Although the
exterior of the cathedral,
built in the 1920s, had
shades of Italianate and
Romanesque design, it did
not conform to any particular architectural style
(demolished 1980).
Declared: 5/6/1970 *(pg. 75)*

HCM #67
CEDAR TREES
Lining both sides of Los Feliz
Boulevard between
Riverside Drive and Western
Avenue, Los Angeles. Two
varieties, *Cedrus Atlantica*
and *Cedrus Deodara*, remain
on Riverside Drive. The trees
were originally planted as
part of a beautification
endeavor, sponsored jointly
by the Los Feliz
Improvement Association
and the Los Feliz Women's
Club in 1916.
Declared: 5/20/1970 *(pg. 290)*

HCM #68
CHARLES LUMMIS
RESIDENCE (*EL ALISAL*)
200 East Avenue 43,
Highland Park. Charles F.
Lummis, author, editor, historian, librarian for the City
of Los Angeles (1905-1910),
archeologist and founder of
the Southwest Museum
(1903), started to build his
unusual home in 1898.
El Alisal, a great stone
house, was largely con-
structed with his own hands
from a set of plans prepared
by his friend, architect
Sumner P. Hunt. It took him
fifteen years to complete
the residence.
Declared: 9/2/1970 *(pg. 169)*

HCM #69
LOS ANGELES ATHLETIC
CLUB BUILDING
431 West 7th Street, Los
Angeles. The club was
founded in 1880. Its present
home, completed in 1912,
was designed in the Beaux
Arts tradition by John
Parkinson and Edwin
Bergstrom. A feature that
received worldwide publicity
upon its completion was the
placement of a 100-foot-
long swimming pool on the
sixth floor rather than in the
basement.
Declared: 9/16/1970 *(pg. 75)*

HCM #70
WIDNEY HALL
650 Childs Way, University of
Southern California Campus,
Los Angeles. The oldest university building in Southern
California, Widney Hall has
been in continuous use for
educational purposes since
its doors were first opened
on October 6, 1880.
Architects E.F. Kysor and
Octavius Morgan designed
the building.
Declared: 12/16/1970 *(pg. 327)*

HCM #71
(Site of) FIRST AFRICAN
METHODIST EPISCOPAL
CHURCH BUILDING
754-762 East 8th Street /
801 South Towne Avenue,
Los Angeles. The First
African Methodist Episcopal
Church was organized in
1872. In 1903 construction
was completed on a Gothic-
style structure based on a
design by English architect
Sir Christopher Wren. The
building was destroyed by
fire on July 4, 1972.
Declared: 1/6/1971 *(pg. 74)*

HCM #72
AUTOMOBILE CLUB OF SOUTHERN CALIFORNIA
2601 South Figueroa Street, Los Angeles. The Automobile Club of Southern California contributed to the economic growth of the City of Los Angeles since it was foremost in the development of suburbs and the decentralization of the area. Sumner P. Hunt and Silas R. Burns designed the headquarters building in 1922, with landscaping by Roland E. Coate. Declared: 2/3/1971 *(pg. 293)*

HCM #73
RESIDENCE
1329 Carroll Avenue, Los Angeles. This circa 1887 Eastlake-style home was built for the area's councilman, Daniel Innes, and was occupied by his family for some thirty years. As the Innes' shoe store prospered downtown, the family became one of the first Blue Book families of Los Angeles.
Declared: 2/3/1971 *(pg. 86)*

HCM #74
RESIDENCE
1345 Carroll Avenue, Los Angeles. Built in 1887 for Michael Sanders, the operator of a storage warehouse, the red brick foundation is characteristic of the Queen Anne style.
Declared: 2/3/1971 *(pg. 83)*

HCM #75
RESIDENCE
1355 Carroll Avenue, Los Angeles. Built in 1887 for capitalist Henry L. Pinney, this house is an example of the relatively unornamented, basic Eastlake style.
Declared: 2/3/1971 *(pg. 86)*

HCM #76
RESIDENCE
1316 Carroll Avenue, Los Angeles. Built circa 1880 in the Eastlake style, the brackets and shell motif below the windows and over the porch steps are noteworthy. Declared: 2/3/1971 *(pg. 83)*

HCM #77
RESIDENCE
1320 Carroll Avenue, Los Angeles. Built circa 1888, this Queen Anne house has turrets, verandas and the generous proportions typical for the period.
Declared: 2/3/1971 *(pg. 84)*

HCM #78
RESIDENCE
1324 Carroll Avenue, Los Angeles. This 1880 Queen Anne cottage is typical of the 19th-century "plan book" houses and exhibits the excellent craftsmanship of its era.
Declared: 2/3/1971 *(pg. 87)*

HCM #79
RESIDENCE
1344 Carroll Avenue, Los Angeles. Built circa 1895, this Gay Nineties house displays noteworthy spindle-and-scroll ornamentation.
Declared: 2/3/1971 *(pg. 87)*

HCM #80
PALM COURT, ALEXANDRIA HOTEL
210 West 5th Street, Los Angeles. True to its original decor, the Palm Court symbolizes the best of the early hospitality of Southern California. A highlight is the magnificent stained glass ceiling extending almost the length of the 196-foot dining room.
Declared: 3/3/1971 *(pg. 76)*

HCM #81
MEMORIAL LIBRARY
4625 West Olympic Boulevard, Los Angeles. Designed by Austin & Ashley, the Tudor and Gothic-inspired Memorial Library was dedicated on April 29, 1930 to commemorate twenty alumni from Los Angeles High School who died in World War I. It was built on land purchased by the alumni association of Los Angeles High School and deeded to the city as a memorial park.
Declared: 4/7/1971 *(pg. 214)*

HCM #82
RIVER STATION AREA/ SOUTHERN PACIFIC RAILROAD
Area bounded by North Broadway, North Spring Street, northward to the Los Angeles River and the southeasterly corner of Elysian Park, and southward to the Capital Milling Company Building, Los Angeles. The area contains many vestiges of 19th-century railroading: freight yards, warehouses, tracks, switch houses, docks and cobblestone pavement.
Declared: 6/16/1971 *(pg. 77)*

HCM #83
BOYLE-BARMORE RESIDENCE
1317 Alvarado Terrace, Los Angeles. Constructed in 1905, it was sold to Edmund H. Barmore, president of the Los Angeles Transfer Co. The residence was designed in the style of English and German chateaux by architect Charles E. Shattuck.
Declared: 7/7/1971 *(pg. 326)*

HCM #84
COHN RESIDENCE
1325 Alvarado Terrace, Los Angeles. Constructed circa 1902 for Morris R. Cohn, the founder of the garment and sportswear industry in Los Angeles, the house was designed in Craftsman Shingle/Chateau style by Hudson & Munsell.
Declared: 7/7/1971 *(pg. 304)*

HCM #85
GILBERT RESIDENCE
1333 Alvarado Terrace, Los Angeles. Constructed circa 1903 for William F. Gilbert, the residence shows unusual utilization of oak and stone, with excellent carving throughout.
Declared: 7/7/1971 *(pg. 294)*

HCM #86
POWERS RESIDENCE
1345 Alvarado Terrace, Los Angeles. Built circa 1904 from a design by architect Arthur L. Haley, it was the residence of Pomeroy Powers, President of the Los Angeles Council from 1900 to 1904. Powers, a real estate developer, was instrumental in establishing the adjacent Terrace Park.
Declared: 7/7/1971 *(pg. 342)*

HCM #87
RAPHAEL RESIDENCE
1353 Alvarado Terrace, Los Angeles. Designed by Sumner P. Hunt and Wesley Eager, this home was constructed circa 1902 for R.H. Raphael, a prominent figure in the glass business in the early 1900s.
Declared: 7/7/1971 *(pg. 307)*

HCM #88
KINNEY-EVERHARDY HOUSE
1401 Alvarado Terrace, Los Angeles. Constructed in 1902, it was designed by Sumner P. Hunt and Wesley Eager for A.W. Kinney, a prominent businessman.
Declared: 7/7/1971 *(pg. 311)*

HCM #89
CENTRAL SPANISH SEVENTH-DAY ADVENTIST CHURCH (formerly First Church of Christ, Scientist)
1366 South Alvarado Street, Los Angeles. Designed by architect Elmer Grey, construction of this Beaux Arts/Italian/Spanish Romanesque edifice began June 10, 1912.
Declared: 7/7/1971 *(pg. 316)*

HCM #90
ST. VINCENT DE PAUL CHURCH
621 West Adams Boulevard, Los Angeles. Built in 1924 and designed by Albert C. Martin, St. Vincent's was the second Roman Catholic church to be consecrated in Los Angeles. The main entrance façade is of stone elaborately carved with statues of saints. The influence of the Spanish Renaissance and California missions can be seen in the furnishings and embellishments of the church.
Declared: 7/21/1971 *(pg. 310)*

HCM #91
KOREAN PHILADELPHIA PRESBYTERIAN CHURCH (formerly Temple Sinai East)
407 South New Hampshire, Los Angeles. Built in 1925, the domed structure, whose grand-style synagogue architecture is described as "eclectic," includes elements of Romanesque, Moorish and "California Hollywood." The building was used as a set in *The Jazz Singer* (1927), the first motion picture produced with an incorporated sound track.
Declared:11/17/1971 *(pg. 386)*

HCM #92
OLD STAGE COACH TRAIL PROPERTY
55 acres immediately south of Chatsworth Park South, north of Oakwood Cemetery, bounded on the west by the Los Angeles City and County lines and on the east by the western terminus of Devonshire Street, Chatsworth. The picturesque Stage Coach Trail dates from the 1860s and represents a significant era in the San Fernando Valley, when it linked Los Angeles, Encino, Simi Valley and Ventura.
Declared: 1/5/1972 *(pg. 255)*

HCM #93
PEPPER TREES
Canoga Avenue from Ventura Boulevard south to Saltillo Street, Woodland Hills. The approximately 300 pepper trees (*Schinus Molle*, native to South America) now growing in the city-owned parkway were planted in the 1920s. They were raised from seed at the nursery owned by Victor Girard of the Boulevard Land Company, owners of most of what is now Woodland Hills.
Declared: 1/5/1972 *(pg. 248)*

HCM #94
PALM TREES AND MEDIAN STRIP
Highland Avenue between Wilshire Boulevard and Melrose Avenue, Los Angeles. In 1928 the residents of Highland Avenue arranged with the city for the planting of palm trees (Queen and *Washingtonia Robusta*) and the construction of the median strip at their own expense.
Declared: 1/26/1972 *(pg. 216)*

HCM #95
RINDGE HOUSE
2263 South Harvard Boulevard, Los Angeles. Completed in 1906 as a residence for Frederick H. Rindge, a financier with extensive land in the West Adams and Malibu areas, the house was designed by Frederick L. Roehrig in the Chateau style.
Declared: 2/23/1972 *(pg. 297)*

HCM #96
STORER HOUSE
8161 Hollywood Boulevard, Hollywood. Built in 1923, it is one of five residences in the Los Angeles designed by Frank Lloyd Wright. This unique house is small but ideally suited to the site.
Declared: 2/23/1972 *(pg. 123)*

HCM #97
(Site of) RESIDENCE
1620 Pleasant Avenue, Boyle Heights. When it was designated, this house was one of the few remaining examples in Los Angeles of what Marcus Whiffen in his American Architecture Since 1780 called "High Victorian Italianate." Following repeated acts of vandalism and a fruitless effort by a private party to relocate it to another site, it was demolished in May 1973.
Declared: 2/23/1972 *(pg. 104)*

HCM #98
MT. PLEASANT HOUSE
Heritage Square, 3800 Homer Street, Los Angeles (original location at 1315 Pleasant Avenue, Boyle Heights). Built in 1876 from a design by the firm of Mathews & Kysor, this grand mansion of High Victorian Italianate architecture was built as a residence for William Hayes Perry, a prominent lumber dealer. The home was moved December 18, 1975.
Declared: 3/15/1972 *(pg. 177)*

HCM #99
RESIDENCE
1036-1038 South Bonnie Brae Street, Los Angeles. Although the architect of this unique structure is unknown, the circa 1896 building has gained wide recognition for its Chateauesque façade.
Declared: 4/5/1972 *(pg. 77)*

HCM #100
GENERAL DOUGLAS MACARTHUR PARK
(formerly Westlake Park)
2230 West 6th Street, Los Angeles. The parkland was acquired by Los Angeles on January 6, 1886 and was named Westlake Park. In 1890 the lake, which had been a neglected pond, was enlarged and in 1896 a bandstand erected. The park was renamed in 1942 at the height of the general's popularity.
Declared: 5/1/1972 *(pg. 387)*

HCM #101
UNION STATION TERMINAL AND LANDSCAPED GROUNDS
800 North Alameda Street, Los Angeles. It was designed by architects John and Donald B. Parkinson, with landscape architect Tommy Tomson. Three of the nation's major railroads, the Southern Pacific, Santa Fe and Union Pacific, pooled their resources in 1933 and proceeded with the construction of the station.
Declared: 8/2/1972 *(pg. 78)*

HCM #102
RESIDENCE
1030 Cesar E. Chavez Avenue, Los Angeles. Built in 1880, this residence is one of the few brick houses of the Victorian era remaining in Los Angeles. Its rich detail includes a broad floor plan unusual for a one-story house, which may indicate a change in the fortune or plans of the builder who cut off his project before it got to the second story.
Declared: 10/4/1972 *(pg. 104)*

HCM #103
FORTHMANN HOUSE AND CARRIAGE HOUSE
2801 South Hoover Street, Los Angeles (original location at 629 West 18th Street). This large 1880s residence is one of the most elegantly detailed Victorian buildings remaining in the city. It was designed by Burgess J. Reeve. The carriage house remained in situ when the house was relocated in 1989.
Declared: 10/4/1972 *(pg. 338)*

HCM #104
COLES P. E. BUFFET/ PACIFIC ELECTRIC BUILDING
118 East 6th Street, Los Angeles. Opened in 1908, the Coles P.E. Buffet is one of the oldest continuously operated restaurants in Los Angeles. The Buffet is located in the Pacific Electric Building, designed by Thornton Fitzhugh in 1903. It was built as the terminal for the horse-drawn trolleys, which later become the largest interurban electrical system in the world, serving Los Angeles, Orange, Riverside and San Bernardino counties.
Declared: 10/18/1972 (restaurant); 10/17/1989 (entire building) *(pg. 78)*

HCM #105
HINER HOUSE
4757 North Figueroa Street, Highland Park. Designed by theater architect Carl Bowler and built for Dr. Edwin C. Hiner, a professor of music, the distinctive architecture of this residence has been described as California chalet with Oriental influence. Stone from the adjacent Arroyo Seco was used in its construction in 1922. A smaller building on this site is known as the "Sousa Nook" because John Phillip Sousa spent much time teaching there.
Declared:11/15/1972 *(pg. 166)*

HCM #106
SAN ENCINO ABBEY
6211 Arroyo Glen, Highland Park. Clyde Browne began construction in 1915 on a place to live, work and be surrounded by the atmosphere of medievalism, which he loved. The original name of this pastiche of a 17th-century monastery was Oldestane Abbey and the materials used included rocks and bits of masonry from old European monasteries, castles and ruined buildings.
Declared:11/15/1972 *(pg. 164)*

HCM #107
McCLURE RESIDENCE
432 North Avenue 66, Garvanza. This example of the mixture of Queen Anne and Eastlake styles was built in 1887; it is attributed to architect Joseph Cather Newsom, who did several designs for the Garvanza Land Company. Owner W.F. McClure was a director of that company.
Declared:11/15/1972 *(pg. 163)*

HCM #108
BEAUDRY AVENUE HOUSE
Heritage Square, 3800 Homer Street, Los Angeles (original location on Beaudry Avenue). The architecture of this 1885 residence has been described as a mixture of Italianate, Eastlake and Queen Anne. The house was relocated in November 1974.
Declared: 1/3/1973 *(pg. 164)*

HCM #109
RESIDENCE
1325 Carroll Avenue, Los Angeles (original location on Court Street). Built in 1887, this residence, moved in March 1978, is almost pure Eastlake in style, but shows elements of the Stick style. The structure has an unusual asymmetrical arrangement of windows and roofline.
Declared: 1/3/1973 *(pg. 88)*

HCM #110
LOS ANGELES POLICE ACADEMY ROCK GARDEN
1880 North Academy Drive, Elysian Park. Early in 1937 François Scotti, an expert landscape artist, was employed to design and build the rock garden, embracing a series of four pools, cascades, a small amphitheater and an outdoor dining area. A large patio, barbecue pit, stairways, walks and recessed stone seats were included. Later alterations were made by the Los Angeles Police Revolver and Athletic Club.
Declared: 1/17/1973 *(pg. 89)*

HCM #111
HOLLYWOOD SIGN
Mount Lee, Hollywood. The sign has long been a symbol of the glamour associated with Hollywood. Built in the fall of 1923, the sign originally read "HOLLYWOOD-LAND" and was constructed as advertising for a subdivision at the top of Beachwood Canyon. Each letter is now constructed of steel and is approximately 50 feet high. The length is 450 feet.
Declared: 2/7/1973 *(pg. 122)*

HCM #112
GABRIELEÑO INDIAN SITE
Fern Dell, Griffith Park, Los Feliz. Archeological surveys discovered sites of villages of the vanished Gabrieleños at the mouth of Fern Dell Canyon, leaving little doubt that fairly large settlements existed in this area and possibly at others that received water from canyons leading from the Hollywood Hills.
Declared: 2/21/1973 *(pg. 276)*

HCM #113
YOUNG'S MARKET BUILDING
1610 West 7th Street, Los Angeles. Constructed in 1924, it was designed by Charles F. Plummer in Greco-Roman style inside and out. This building is one of the better examples of this style in Los Angeles. The exterior grillwork, marble and the ceramic polychrome frieze are particularly well executed.
Declared: 3/7/1973 *(pg. 292)*

HCM #114
WILSHIRE UNITED METHODIST CHURCH
4350 Wilshire Boulevard, Los Angeles. Dedicated in 1924 and designed by Allison & Allison, this church stands as a magnificent edifice. Its interior and exterior concrete construction exhibit Romanesque and Gothic influence.
Declared: 3/7/1973 *(pg. 404)*

HCM #115
EVANS RESIDENCE (SUNSHINE HALL)
419 South Lorraine Boulevard, Los Angeles. Designed for Mrs. Jeanette Donovan by architect I. Eisner circa 1910, the house is a rare Southern California example of the Classical Revival initiated in the eastern United States. The exterior is dominated by a Roman temple portico and Ionic columns.
Declared: 3/21/1973 *(pg. 397)*

HCM #116
WILSHIRE BOULEVARD TEMPLE
3663 Wilshire Boulevard, Los Angeles. Dedicated in 1929, this imposing Byzantine-inspired temple is one of the largest and most influential Reform synagogues. The notable interior features symbolic murals by Hugo Ballin, depicting episodes in the biblical and post-biblical history of the Hebrew people. The architects were A.M. Edelman, S. Tilden Norton and David C. Allison.
Declared: 3/21/1973 *(pg. 393)*

HCM #117
RESIDENCE
2218 South Harvard Boulevard, Los Angeles. Reportedly built in 1905, the architecture of this beautiful residence has been described as American Colonial.
Declared: 4/4/1973 *(pg. 308)*

HCM #118
PELLISSIER BUILDING
3780 Wilshire Boulevard, Los Angeles. Designed by Morgan, Walls & Clements, construction began in October 1930. The blue-green, terra-cotta-covered tower is described as French Zigzag Moderne. Its ornate Wiltern Theatre, with an interior by G. Albert Lansburgh, held the largest theater pipe organ in the western United States.
Declared: 8/16/1973 *(pg. 224)*

HCM #119
COHN-GOLDWATER BUILDING
525 East 12th Street, Los Angeles. In 1909 Morris Cohn and Lemuel Goldwater, garment manufacturers, built the first modern, Class-A, steel-reinforced-concrete factory building in Los Angeles at a cost of $150,000. It is now used for storage.
Declared: 8/16/1973 *(pg. 78)*

HCM #120
SAINT SOPHIA CATHEDRAL
1324 South Normandie Avenue, Los Angeles. The late theater mogul Charles P. Skouras was one of the chief motivators for the construction of this magnificent cathedral dedicated in September 1952. In keeping with Byzantine tradition, it is almost totally devoid of exterior ornamentation. The richly decorated interior was designed by Kalionzes, Klingerman & Walker.
Declared: 6/6/1973 *(pg. 298)*

HCM #121
GARFIELD BUILDING
403 West 8th Street, Los Angeles. Constructed in 1928 and designed by Claude Beelman, it is a significant example of the opulent Art Deco style.
Declared: 8/22/1973 (lobby); 3/17/1982 (entire building) *(pg. 79)*

HCM #122
BUCK HOUSE
805 South Genesee Avenue, Los Angeles. It was designed in 1934 by architect R.M. Schindler in the Streamline Moderne style.
Declared: 3/20/1974 *(pg. 218)*

HCM #123
LOVELL HEALTH HOUSE
4616 Dundee Drive, Los Angeles. Designed in 1929 by architect Richard J. Neutra in the International Style, this home represents one of the earliest residential uses of the all-steel frame.
Declared: 3/30/1974 *(pg. 277)*

HCM #124
TIERMAN HOUSE
2323 Micheltorena Street, Silver Lake. Completed in 1940, the residence was designed by Gregory Ain.
Declared: 4/3/1974 *(pg. 276)*

HCM #125
FINE ARTS BUILDING
811 West 7th Street, Los Angeles. Completed in 1925 and designed by the firm of Walker & Eisen, the Fine Arts Building is an excellent example of the Romanesque style.
Declared: 4/17/1974 *(pg. 28)*

HCM #126
FRANKLIN AVENUE BRIDGE (SHAKESPEARE BRIDGE)
Franklin Avenue at St. George Street, Los Angeles. A picturesque span with Gothic arches and turrets built in the 1920s, this bridge has been used in numerous films including *The Wizard of Oz.*
Declared: 4/17/1974 *(pg. 279)*

HCM #127
EXPOSITION CLUB HOUSE
3990 South Menlo Avenue, Los Angeles. Part of the complex of recreational buildings in Exposition Park, this Spanish Colonial Revival building has served the community since the 1920s.
Declared: 5/1/1974 *(pg. 295)*

HCM #128
HANCOCK MEMORIAL MUSEUM
University of Southern California, University Avenue at Childs Way, Los Angeles. The four formal rooms and foyer were part of a twenty-three-room mansion built by the Hancock family at the northeast corner of Vermont Avenue and Wilshire Boulevard in the late 19th century.
Declared: 5/15/1974 *(pg. 302)*

HCM #129
RESIDENCE
767 Garland Avenue, Los Angeles. A Queen Anne mansion built for oil executive Charles C. L. Leslie, it was designed by Dennis & Farwell.
Declared: 6/19/1974 *(pg. 409)*

HCM #130
SAMUEL-NOVARRO HOUSE
5609 Valley Oak Drive, Hollywood Hills. This Art Deco residence was designed by architect Lloyd Wright in 1928.
Declared: 7/17/1974 *(pg. 122)*

HCM #131
DUNBAR HOTEL (formerly the Somerville Hotel)
4225 South Central Avenue, Los Angeles. Completed in 1928, it is listed on the National Register of Historic Places due to its ties to African American heritage.
Declared: 8/4/1974 *(pg. 28)*

HCM #132
STONEY POINT OUTCROPPINGS
North Chatsworth. A natural site east of Topanga Canyon Boulevard, it is one of the most picturesque areas in Los Angeles.
Declared:11/20/1974 *(pg. 239)*

HCM #133
MINNIE HILL PALMER RESIDENCE
Chatsworth Park South Chatsworth. Built in 1913, this little ranch cottage is typical of those built by the homesteaders of the San Fernando Valley.
Declared:11/20/1974 *(pg. 248)*

HCM #134
CROSSROADS OF THE WORLD
6671 West Sunset Boulevard, Hollywood. A complex of buildings designed by Robert V. Derrah in 1937. The central building is in the form of a ship, while the surrounding structures are in a variety of European styles. It was a prominent shopping center in the 1930s.
Declared:12/4/1974 *(pg. 123)*

HCM #135
CANOGA MISSION GALLERY
23130 Sherman Way, Canoga Park. This 1936 Mission stable was converted to a community center.
Declared:12/4/1974 *(pg. 234)*

HCM #136
ST. MARY OF THE ANGELS CHURCH
4510 Finley Avenue, Hollywood. Designed by Carleton Winslow, Sr. in 1930, this Spanish Revival church is described as a little jewel of architecture.
Declared:12/4/1974 *(pg. 278)*

HCM #137
FINNEY'S CAFETERIA (formerly The Chocolate Shoppe)
217 West 6th Street, Los Angeles. This 1914 structure features an interior with Ernest A. Batchelder tiles.
Declared: 1/15/1975 *(pg. 29)*

HCM #138
COCA-COLA BUILDING
1334 South Central Avenue, Los Angeles. A Streamline Moderne building designed by Robert V. Derrah in 1939, the ship-like structure, replete with portholes, a catwalk, cargo doors and topped by a bridge, encloses of four older buildings.
Declared: 2/5/1975 *(pg. 31)*

HCM #139
SHRINE AUDITORIUM
665 West Jefferson Boulevard, Los Angeles. Designed by John C. Austin (exterior) and G. Albert Lansburgh (interior), construction was completed in January 1926. It ranks among the largest theaters in the United States with a seating capacity of 6,700.
Declared: 3/5/1975 *(pg. 313)*

HCM #140
CAST IRON COMMERCIAL BUILDING
740-748 South San Pedro Street, Los Angeles. This 1903 structure is one of the best examples in Los Angeles of buildings made with prefabricated metal.
Declared: 3/19/1975 *(pg. 32)*

HCM #141
CHATSWORTH RESERVOIR KILN SITE
Southeasterly from the intersection of Woolsey Canyon Road and Valley Circle Boulevard, Chatsworth. The kiln provided bricks and tiles for the San Fernando Mission.
Declared: 4/2/1975 *(pg. 233)*

HCM #142
EL MIO
5905 El Mio Drive, Highland Park. An imposing Queen Anne residence constructed circa 1890, the home was built for Los Angeles Superior Court Judge David P. Hatch.
Declared: 4/16/1975 *(pg. 189)*

HCM #143
RESIDENCE
6028 Hayes Avenue, Highland Park. Circa 1885, the outstanding feature of this Queen Anne residence is the veranda, which crosses its simple façade.
Declared: 4/16/1975 *(pg. 166)*

HCM #144
RESIDENCE
2054 Griffin Avenue, Lincoln Heights. Built circa 1887, it is unusual for Queen Anne ornamentation to be used in a masonry house.
Declared: 5/21/1975 *(pg. 105)*

HCM #145
RESIDENCE
3537 Griffin Avenue, Lincoln Heights. The residence, circa 1886, is described as Queen Anne with Italianate elements.
Declared: 5/21/1975 *(pg. 106)*

HCM #146
MUNICIPAL FERRY BUILDING (LOS ANGELES MARITIME MUSEUM)
Berth 84, foot of 6th Street, San Pedro. Built in 1941, it accommodated ferryboats carrying workers between San Pedro and Terminal Island. The Maritime Museum is open to the public.
Declared: 9/17/1975 *(pg. 262)*

HCM #147
JAMES H. DODSON RESIDENCE
859 West 13th Street, San Pedro. Constructed in 1885, this residence is one of San Pedro's finest examples of Victorian architecture.
Declared: 8/17/1975 *(pg. 274)*

HCM #148
CORAL TREES
Median strip of San Vicente Boulevard between 26th Street and Bringham Avenue, Brentwood. This area is landscaped with coral trees (*Erythrina Caffra*), the official tree of the City of Los Angeles.
Declared: 1/7/1976 *(pg. 360)*

HCM #149
ENNIS HOUSE
2607 Glendower Avenue, Hollywood. Built in 1924, the Ennis residence has been described as the most monumental of Frank Lloyd Wright's western experiments with concrete textile block construction.
Declared: 3/3/1976 *(pg. 278)*

HCM #150
LOS ANGELES CITY HALL
200 North Spring Street, Los Angeles. Completed in 1928, architects John C. Austin, Albert C. Martin and John Parkinson used a classical temple as inspiration for a base that supports a 28-story tower that has become a symbol of the city. The interior public spaces are Byzantine in ornamentation.
Declared: 3/24/1976 *(pg. 29)*

HCM #151
CHATEAU MARMONT
8221 West Sunset Boulevard, Hollywood. Constructed circa 1926 by Arnold Weitzman, this hotel has long been associated with movie stars.
Declared: 3/24/1976 *(pg. 125)*

HCM #152
FAITH BIBLE CHURCH (formerly Norwegian Lutheran Church)
18531 Gresham Street, Northridge. The church was built in 1917 in the Gothic style in Zelzah, which later became Northridge.
Declared: 4/7/1976 *(pg. 242)*

HCM #153
(Site of) LINCOLN PARK CAROUSEL
Mission Road and Valley Boulevard, Los Angeles. Designed by Oliver and Ross Davis in 1914, the Carousel was burned by vandals on August 25, 1976.
Declared: 4/21/1976 *(pg. 109)*

HCM #154
FIREBOAT No. 2 AND (site of) FIREHOUSE No. 112
Berth 227, foot of Old Dock Street, San Pedro. Fireboat No. 2, known as "the grand old lady" of the fire department fleet, was launched October 20, 1925. Firehouse No. 112 served as its home base. Although the fireboat still remains, the firehouse was demolished in 1984.
Declared: 5/5/1976 *(pg. 264)*

HCM #155
MEMORY CHAPEL, CALVARY PRESBYTERIAN CHURCH
1160 North Marine Avenue, Wilmington. Constructed in 1870, it is the oldest Protestant church in the harbor area.
Declared: 5/5/1976 *(pg. 265)*

HCM #156
FIRE STATION No. 1
2230 Pasadena Avenue, Lincoln Heights. Built in 1940, it is a sterling example of Streamline Moderne architecture.
Declared: 7/7/1976 *(pg. 106)*

HCM #157
RESIDENCE
3110 North Broadway, Lincoln Heights. Built circa 1880, this residence is an excellent example of the Queen Anne style. Declared: 7/7/1976 *(pg. 108)*

HCM #158
MARY ANDREWS CLARK RESIDENCE OF THE Y.W.C.A.
306 Loma Drive, Los Angeles. Built by Senator William Andrews Clark of Montana in 1913 as a memorial to his mother, its interiors, with beautiful woodwork, marble, tile and art glass, are a tribute to the fine craftsmanship of the early 20th century. It was designed by Arthur B. Benton in the French Chateau style. Declared: 7/7/1976 *(pg. 406)*

HCM #159
RALPH J. BUNCHE HOME
1221 East 40th Place, Los Angeles. Dr. Bunche, the first African American Nobel Peace Prize recipient, lived in this house during his youth when he attended 30th Street School, Jefferson High School and UCLA. Declared: 7/27/1976 *(pg. 31)*

HCM #160
MANZANAR
Highway 395, Inyo County. Located 225 miles north of metropolitan Los Angeles, Manzanar was a World War II relocation center, confining 10,000 persons of Japanese ancestry, many from the City of Los Angeles, from March 1942 to December 1945. Declared: 9/15/1976 *(pg. 419)*

HCM #161
WOLFER PRINTING COMPANY BUILDING
416 Wall Street, Los Angeles. Built in 1929 and patterned after a 19th-century English print shop, this is an outstanding example of Tudor Revival, designed by Edward Cray Taylor and Ellis Wing Taylor. Declared: 9/15/1976 *(pg. 32)*

HCM #162
WILLIAM MULHOLLAND MEMORIAL FOUNTAIN
Los Feliz Boulevard and Riverside Drive, Los Angeles. Dedicated on August 1, 1940 and designed by Walter S. Clayberg, it honors William Mulholland (1855-1935) as "Father of the Los Angeles Municipal Water System." Declared:10/6/1976 *(pg. 282)*

HCM #163
(Site of) FIRST WALT DISNEY STUDIO
2725 Hyperion Avenue, Los Angeles. Although a market now occupies the land, this was the site of Walt and Roy Disney's first formal studio in 1926. *Snow White and the Seven Dwarfs* (1937), the first feature-length animated film, was produced at this location. Declared:10/6/1976 *(pg. 285)*

HCM #164
GLENDALE-HYPERION BRIDGE
Spanning the Los Angeles River, the Golden State Freeway and Riverside Drive, between Ettrick Street and Glenfeliz Boulevard, Los Angeles. Constructed of a series of reinforced-concrete arches, it was completed February 25, 1929. It has a total length of 1,370 feet and road width of 56 feet. Declared:10/20/1976 *(pg. 279)*

HCM #165
FIRE STATION No. 27
1355 North Cahuenga Boulevard, Hollywood. When it was built in 1930, this 22,000-square-foot building was the largest fire station west of the Mississippi. It was designed by Peter K. Schabarum. Open to the public. Declared:10/20/1976 *(pg. 156)*

HCM #166
CARRIAGE HOUSE
1417 Kellam Avenue, Los Angeles. Built in 1880, it is the best remaining example of a Victorian-era carriage house. It contains wood shingles of various designs, vertical and horizontal siding and diagonal braces. Declared:11/3/1976 *(pg. 89)*

HCM #167
RESIDENCE
826 South Coronado, Los Angeles (originally located at 633 West 15th Street). This is a rare example of Queen Anne architecture in the Caribbean style. Declared:11/17/1976 *(pg. 403)*

HCM #168
GRIFFITH OBSERVATORY
2800 East Observatory Road, Griffith Park. Designed by John C. Austin and F.M. Ashley, it opened May 14, 1935 to provide public access to the cosmic discoveries of astronomy and modern science. The structure is a fine example of Art Deco architecture. Declared:11/17/1976 *(pg. 280)*

HCM #169
RESIDENCE OF WILLIAM GRANT STILL
1262 Victoria Avenue, Los Angeles. In 1936, William Grant Still was the first African American to conduct a major symphony orchestra in the United States. He has to his credit at least 150 compositions in many forms. His work continues to be performed by top-ranking conductors and musical organizations throughout the world.
Declared:12/1/1976 *(pg. 336)*

HCM #170
PAUL R. WILLIAMS RESIDENCE
1690 Victoria Avenue, Los Angeles. This home was designed in the International Moderne style in 1952. Williams, an African American architect, earned renown as a designer of thousands of private residences throughout the United States and South America. He created homes for such celebrities as Frank Sinatra, Danny Thomas, Tyrone Power and Cary Grant. His commissions include the Music Corporation of America's office building in Beverly Hills and the Los Angeles Courthouse.
Declared:12/1/1976 *(pg. 299)*

HCM #171
(Site of) TIMMS' LANDING
San Pedro Harbor, northwest end of fish slip, landscaped park in the front of Fisherman's Co-op building, east of the harbor belt railroad tracks, San Pedro. In the mid-1800s it was the wharf for Los Angeles's first harbor. No structures remain of the cluster of buildings or the jetty.
Declared: 2/16/1977 *(pg. 267)*

HCM #172
STONEHURST RECREATION CENTER BUILDING
9901 Dronfield Avenue, Sun Valley. This building was constructed circa 1930 of native stone by Montelongo, an Indian stonemason who with his helpers laid the round and smooth rock picked up in the local area.
Declared: 3/9/1977 *(pg. 258)*

HCM #173
WELSH PRESBYTERIAN CHURCH BUILDING
1153 South Valencia Street, Los Angeles. Dedicated on September 5, 1890, it was designed by S. Tilden Norton as the first synagogue structure of the Sinai congregation. This Greek Revival building has an interior of exceptional quality. In 1926 the Jewish congregation sold the property to Welsh Presbyterian Church.
Declared: 4/20/1977 *(pg. 32)*

HCM #174
VILLAGE GREEN (formerly Baldwin Hills Village)
5112-5595 Village Green, Baldwin Hills. Completed in 1942, this urban housing complex received the American Institute of Architects award for architectural design of enduring significance in 1972. The architects were Reginald D. Johnson, Wilson & Merrill and Robert E. Alexander.
Declared: 5/4/1977 *(pg. 17)*

HCM #175
Y.W.C.A. HOLLYWOOD STUDIO CLUB
1215 Lodi Place, Hollywood. Designed by architect Julia Morgan, the Studio Club opened May 7, 1926 offering low-cost housing for young women hoping to make it in the movies. Among its residents were Marilyn Monroe and Kim Novak.
Declared: 5/4/1977 *(pg. 125)*

HCM #176
RESIDENCE
1321 Carroll Avenue, Los Angeles (originally located at 1145 Court Street). This 1880s residence has an unusual isometric arrangement of the windows and roofline.
Declared: 7/13/1977 *(pg. 90)*

HCM #177
SUBWAY TERMINAL BUILDING
417 South Hill Street, Los Angeles. Constructed in 1925 and designed by Schultze & Weaver, this Beaux Arts structure was the only subway terminal in downtown Los Angeles. At its peak in 1944, the Pacific Electric Railway carried approximately 65,000 passengers on 844 trains daily.
Declared: 7/27/1977 *(pg. 35)*

HCM #178
HERALD-EXAMINER BUILDING
1111 South Broadway, Los Angeles. This 1915 building by Julia Morgan is an example of Spanish Colonial Revival architecture.
Declared: 8/17/1977 *(pg. 36)*

HCM #179
(Site of) RESIDENCE
919 West 20th Street, Los Angeles (original location at the corner of Oak and Washington Streets). Built in 1908, it was moved to this site in 1918. It was badly damaged by fire in May 1978 and demolished the same year.
Declared: 8/17/1977 *(pg. 347)*

HCM #180

(Site of) FILMING OF THE FIRST TALKING FEATURE FILM

5800 West Sunset Boulevard, Los Angeles. In October 1927 *The Jazz Singer,* the first feature film with synchronized dialogue, was shot in a studio at this location.
Declared: 9/21/1977 *(pg. 124)*

HCM #181

BURIAL PLACE OF J.B. LANKERSHIM

North end of Nichols Canyon Road, Los Angeles. Born March 24, 1850, James B. Lankershim was one of the subdividers of the San Fernando Valley.
Declared: 1/18/1978 *(pg. 236)*

HCM #182

IVY SUBSTATION

9015 Venice Boulevard, Los Angeles. Completed in July 1907, the substation provided power for the expanding Los Angeles Pacific Railway system. Its architecture is described as Mission Revival.
Declared: 2/1/1978 *(pg. 380)*

HCM #183

(Site of) WEST FAÇADE OF THE PAN PACIFIC AUDITORIUM

7600 Beverly Boulevard, Los Angeles. Designed in 1935 by Welton Becket and Walter Wurdeman, the Pan Pacific was a premier example of Streamline Moderne. All but the west façade was destroyed by fire in 1989, and the entire building had to be demolished in 1992.
Declared: 3/1/1978 *(pg. 215)*

HCM #184

TOWER OF WOODEN PALLETS

15357 Magnolia Boulevard, Van Nuys. Constructed by Daniel Van Meter in 1951 of approximately 2,000 3×3×6-foot wooden pallets, it has a 22-foot circumference at its base and purportedly sits atop the grave of a child buried in 1869.
Declared: 4/19/1978 *(pg. 243)*

HCM #185

(Site of) PRESIDENT'S HOUSE (formerly Pepperdine University, Los Angeles)

7851 Budlong Avenue, Los Angeles. Built in 1912, the interior of the building was significant for its tile work and hardware crafted in the Mission style.
Declared: 4/19/1978 *(pg. 303)*

HCM #186

MORGAN HOUSE (HARBOR AREA Y.W.C.A.)

437 West 9th Street, San Pedro. This Craftsman building was designed by Julia Morgan.
Declared: 5/3/1978 *(pg. 267)*

HCM #187

KOREAN BELL AND BELFRY OF FRIENDSHIP

Angel's Gate Park, Gaffey and 37th Streets, San Pedro. A gift from the people of the Republic of Korea in commemoration of the United States Bicentennial, the bell was designed by Kim Se-jung and was patterned after the largest Oriental bell in existence, the bronze bell of King Songdok. It was dedicated on October 3, 1976.
Declared: 5/3/1978 *(pg. 260)*

HCM #188

U.S.S. *LOS ANGELES* NAVAL MONUMENT

John S. Gibson, Jr. Park, Harbor Boulevard between 5th and 6th Streets, San Pedro. Designed by Terryle Smeed and dedicated in 1977 to the men and ships of the United States Navy, it features a 70-foot concrete platform housing the mainmast, bow, anchors, bollards and anchor capstan cover of the heavy cruiser U.S.S. *Los Angeles.*
Declared: 5/3/1978 *(pg. 266)*

HCM #189

RESIDENCE

1407 Carroll Avenue, Los Angeles. Constructed in 1885, the design was by architect Joseph Cather Newsom.
Declared: 5/3/1978 *(pg. 90)*

HCM #190

RESIDENCE AND CARRIAGE HOUSE

1411 Carroll Avenue, Los Angeles. Built in 1885 with a mixture of Eastlake and Queen Anne details, this residence boasts an original carriage house and superior interior plaster and woodwork.
Declared: 5/3/1978 *(pg. 92)*

HCM #191

RESIDENCE

1441-1443 1/2 Carroll Avenue, Los Angeles. This Queen Anne building was erected as a residence for James S. Luckenbach in 1887. It was sold in 1902 to Kaspare Cohn (the founder of Union Bank) who established the building as the Kaspare Cohn Hospital, the forerunner to Cedars of Lebanon Hospital.
Declared: 5/3/1978 *(pg. 90)*

HCM #192
(Site of) FRANKLIN GARDEN APARTMENTS
6917-6933 Franklin Avenue, Hollywood. Designed by L.H. Baldwin in 1920, this Hollywood landmark was an outstanding example of California Spanish architecture incorporating beautiful landscaping (demolished 1978).
Declared: 6/7/1978 *(pg. 124)*

HCM #193
PANTAGES THEATRE
6233 Hollywood Boulevard, Hollywood. Designed in 1929 by architect B. Marcus Priteca and interior decorator Anthony Heinsbergen, the theater is an exceptional example of 1920s Art Deco design. Opened on June 4, 1930 as the last and largest in a chain of theaters operated by vaudeville magnate Alexander Pantages, the interior is considered by many to be one of the most magnificent examples of theater architecture in Los Angeles.
Declared: 7/5/1978 *(pg. 127)*

HCM #194
HOLLYWOOD WALK OF FAME
Hollywood Boulevard between Gower Street and Sycamore Avenue and Vine Street between Yucca Street and Sunset Boulevard, Hollywood. Conceived by the Hollywood Chamber of Commerce in the late 1950s, the "Walk" is a tribute to the artists who have made significant contributions to the film, radio, television and recording industries. It contains over 2,500 bronze stars embedded in charcoal terrazzo squares, each with its distinctive emblem identifying the category in which the recipient is being honored.
Declared: 7/5/1978 *(pg. 157)*

HCM #195
OVIATT BUILDING
617 South Olive Street, Los Angeles. Designed by Joseph Feil of Feil & Paradise and opened in 1928, the building is recognized as a superb example of Art Deco design. The building features outstanding works by the French glass maker René Lalique.
Declared: 7/19/1978 *(pg. 30)*

HCM #196
VARIETY ARTS CENTER BUILDING
940 South Figueroa Street, Los Angeles. Built in 1924 as a stately five-story Italian Renaissance theater and clubhouse, it was designed by the firm Allison & Allison for the Friday Morning Club, a woman's group established in 1891.
Declared: 8/9/1978 *(pg. 36)*

HCM #197
BRITT MANSION AND FORMAL GARDENS
2141 West Adams Boulevard, Los Angeles. Completed in 1910, this Classical Revival residence was designed by A. F. Rosenheim for attorney Eugene W. Britt. It now functions as the headquarters of the Amateur Athletic Foundation of Los Angeles. Open to the public.
Declared: 8/23/1978 *(pg. 324)*

HCM #198
KCET STUDIOS
4401 West Sunset Boulevard, Los Angeles. The site has been the home of several motion picture companies including Monogram and Allied Artists. The Keystone Kops, Charlie Chaplin and Fatty Arbuckle made movies here. It has been the home of KCET, a public broadcast station, since 1971.
Declared: 9/20/1978 *(pg. 155)*

HCM #199
DAVID FAMILIAN CHAPEL OF TEMPLE ADAT ARI EL
5540 Laurel Canyon Boulevard, North Hollywood. Dedicated on November 7, 1949, the chapel is the first purpose-built synagogue in the San Fernando Valley. The temple congregation dates from 1938.
Declared: 9/20/1978 *(pg. 250)*

HCM #200
SECOND BAPTIST CHURCH BUILDING
2412 Griffith Avenue, Los Angeles. Constructed in 1925 and designed by architect Paul R. Williams, the building is recognized for its historical significance and is an example of the Lombard Romanesque style of the 1920s. The church has been the hub of the cultural life in the African American community since its inception in 1885.
Declared:10/18/1978 *(pg. 320)*

HCM #201
VAN NUYS WOMAN'S CLUB BUILDING
14836 Sylvan Street, Van Nuys. Constructed in 1917 as a Craftsman style building, the club, founded in 1912, is one of the oldest social institutions in the San Fernando Valley.
Declared:10/18/1978 *(pg. 244)*

HCM #202
VALLEY MUNICIPAL BUILDING
(VAN NUYS CITY HALL)
14410 Sylvan Street, Van Nuys. Constructed in 1932 and designed by Peter K. Schabarum, this landmark is a good example of French Zigzag Moderne.
Declared:10/18/1978 *(pg. 245)*

HCM #203
BAIRD HOUSE
14603 Hamlin Street, Van Nuys. Built in 1921 for the family of Robert J. Baird, owner of the Van Nuys Nursery Company, this bungalow is now the property of the Volunteer League of the San Fernando Valley. Declared:10/18/1978 *(pg. 255)*

HCM #204
LEDERER RESIDENCE AND IMMEDIATE ENVIRONS
23134 Sherman Way, Canoga Park. Beginning in 1934, the house was constructed over a period of years with the help of builder John R. Litke. Materials were chosen with care and employed in such a manner as to make them appear old. It is a distinguished example of Mission Revival. Declared:11/15/1978 *(pg. 235)*

HCM #205
LOS ANGELES STOCK EXCHANGE BUILDING
618 South Spring Street, Los Angeles. Designed by Samuel E. Lunden and opened for business on January 5, 1931, it is an outstanding example of Classical Moderne architecture. Special recognition is given to the interior of the building with its bronze doors, cove lighting and ceiling murals. Declared: 1/3/1979 *(pg. 33)*

HCM #206
RESIDENCE
724 East Edgeware Road, Los Angeles. Built in 1887, this Victorian residence is noteworthy for its mansard tower, ornamental ironwork and fish-scale shingles. Declared: 1/3/1979 *(pg. 91)*

HCM #207
RESIDENCE
1334 Kellam Avenue, Los Angeles. Built circa 1890, this residence is an excellent example of Queen Anne architecture with Colonial Revival influence. Declared: 1/17/1979 *(pg. 93)*

HCM #208
RESIDENCE AND CARRIAGE HOUSE
845 South Lake Street, Los Angeles. Constructed in 1902 for Mrs. Susana Machado Bernard, this opulent home was designed by architect John B. Parkinson. Declared: 1/17/1979 *(pg. 300)*

HCM #209
WILSHIRE CHRISTIAN CHURCH BUILDING
634 South Normandie Avenue, Los Angeles. Built from 1922 to 1923, this church was designed by architect Robert H. Orr in a Northern Italian Romanesque style. Orr was one of the outstanding church architects in the Los Angeles area. Declared: 1/17/1979 *(pg. 399)*

HCM #210
TERRACE PARK AND POWERS PLACE
Powers Place and 14th Street, Los Angeles. This 1.17-acre site was dedicated for public use on August 22, 1904. The Terrace Park area is an integral part of the Alvarado Terrace complex. The brick paving of Powers Place recalls the era when horse-drawn vehicles were prevalent. Declared: 2/21/1979 *(pg. 317)*

HCM #211
GRANITE BLOCK PAVING
Bruno Street between Alameda and North Main Streets, Los Angeles. This short industrial street, just north of the Civic Center and southwest of Chinatown, is the last surviving street in Los Angeles with the original paving of hand-hewn granite blocks. Declared: 3/7/1979 *(pg. 35)*

HCM #212
STIMSON RESIDENCE
2421 South Figueroa Street, Los Angeles. Built in 1891 and designed by architect Carroll H. Brown, the residence is a rare example of Richardsonian Romanesque architecture in Los Angeles. Declared: 5/16/1979 *(pg. 337)*

HCM #213
S.S. *CATALINA* (THE GREAT WHITE STEAMSHIP)
Port of Ensenada, Mexico. Built in 1924 by William Wrigley, it carried more than 25 million passengers between San Pedro and Avalon, Santa Catalina Island from 1924 until 1975. The ship was taken to Ensenada, Mexico in 1985 and served as a floating restaurant and retail center until 1997, when it began to sink at its mooring and was abandoned. Declared: 5/16/1979 *(pg. 418)*

HCM #214
MT. CARMEL HIGH SCHOOL BUILDING
7011 South Hoover Street, Los Angeles. Constructed in 1934, the building is an excellent example of Spanish architecture and is the first school in Los Angeles constructed to building codes enacted following the 1932 earthquake. It was operated by the Catholic Fathers of the Order of Mt. Carmel for many years. Declared: 6/6/1979 *(pg. 406)*

HCM #215
BOB'S MARKET
1234 Bellevue Avenue, Los Angeles. This building is an example of a 1910 neighborhood grocery store with unusual Oriental details.
Declared: 6/6/1979 *(pg. 93)*

HCM #216
RESIDENCE
917 Douglas Street, Los Angeles. Constructed circa 1887, this residence is an example of Eastlake architecture.
Declared: 6/6/1979 *(pg. 92)*

HCM #217
RESIDENCE
1101 Douglas Street, Los Angeles. This Queen Anne residence was purportedly built for Moses Langley Wicks, an insurance man from Missouri.
Declared: 6/6/1979 *(pg. 94)*

HCM #218
RESIDENCE
945 East Edgeware Road, Los Angeles. Built circa 1908, this residence is an example of Craftsman architecture.
Declared: 6/6/1979 *(pg. 95)*

HCM #219
RESIDENCE
1239 Boston Street, Los Angeles. Built circa 1887, this distinguished Queen Anne residence has beautiful spool work and decorative shingles.
Declared: 6/6/1979 *(pg. 80)*

HCM #220
RESIDENCE
1343 Kellam Avenue, Los Angeles. Built circa 1887, this Queen Anne residence features shingles in diamond and circular patterns.
Declared: 6/6/1979 *(pg. 97)*

HCM #221
RESIDENCE AND CARRIAGE HOUSE
1347 Kellam Avenue, Los Angeles. Built circa 1887, this Queen Anne residence is nearly identical to the residence at 1343 Kellam Avenue (HCM #220).
Declared: 6/6/1979 *(pg. 96)*

HCM #222
RESIDENCE
1405 Kellam Avenue, Los Angeles. Built circa 1905, it is an example of Mission Revival architecture.
Declared: 6/6/1979 *(pg. 100)*

HCM #223
RESIDENCE
824 East Kensington Road, Los Angeles (original location at Angelina and Boylston Streets). Built in 1894 for contractor Z.H. Weller, this residence is an excellent example of Queen Anne architecture with traces of Eastlake and Moorish influence. When oil wells began to proliferate around it circa 1909, it was moved to this location.
Declared: 6/20/1979 *(pg. 95)*

HCM #224
MACY STREET VIADUCT
Cesar E. Chavez Avenue, crossing the Los Angeles River between Mission Road and Vignes Street, Los Angeles. Built in 1926, this viaduct is Spanish Colonial in design. It features Ionic and Doric columns with unique post lights. Macy Street was named for Dr. Obed Macy, an early Los Angeles physician.
Declared: 8/1/1979 *(pg. 112)*

HCM #225
LOS ANGELES THEATRE
615 South Broadway, Los Angeles. The Baroque building was designed by Los Angeles theater architect S. Charles Lee. It opened on January 30, 1931.
Declared: 8/15/1979 *(pg. 34)*

HCM #226
(Site of) MASQUERS CLUB BUILDING
1765 North Sycamore Avenue, Hollywood. Built in the late 1920s, the Tudor Revival residence housed one of Hollywood's oldest and most respected theatrical clubs. Originally the home of silent screen star Antonio Moreno, the building contained priceless theatrical memorabilia (demolished 1985).
Declared: 8/29/1979 *(pg. 140)*

HCM #227
JANES HOUSE
6541 Hollywood Boulevard, Hollywood. Built in 1902 and designed by Oliver Dennis and Lyman Farwell in the Queen Anne style, it was purchased by the Janes family in 1903. For many years, the Janes sisters, Carrie, Mabel and Grace, operated the Misses Janes Kindergarten in their home. Children from the Hollywood community, including those of Cecil B. DeMille and Charles Chaplin, attended this school.
Declared: 4/3/1980 *(pg. 127)*

HCM #228
LAURELWOOD APARTMENTS
11833-11837 Laurelwood Drive, Studio City. Built in 1948, this complex was designed by architect R.M. Schindler.
Declared: 4/22/1980 *(pg. 256)*

HCM #229
WESTMINSTER PRESBYTERIAN CHURCH
2230 West Jefferson Boulevard, Los Angeles. Built for the first African American Presbyterian congregation in Los Angeles, the church was founded in 1904 and was the largest of its denomination in the West.
Declared: 6/11/1980 *(pg. 328)*

HCM #230
VILLA MARIA
2425 South Western Avenue, Los Angeles. Built circa 1908 and designed by F.L. Roehrig, this house is a distinguished example of the Tudor Revival style.
Declared: 6/12/1980 *(pg. 297)*

HCM #231
EL GRECO APARTMENTS
817 North Haywood, Los Angeles (original location at 1028 Tiverton Avenue, Westwood). Built circa 1929 and designed by F. Pierpont Davis and Walter S. Davis, this Spanish Colonial Revival apartment building was relocated in 1985.
Declared: 6/30/1980 *(pg. 353)*

HCM #232
DEPARTMENT OF WATER AND POWER BUILDING
5108 Lankershim Boulevard, North Hollywood. Built circa 1939 and designed by architect S. Charles Lee, this building is an outstanding example of Streamline Moderne architecture.
Declared: 7/14/1980 *(pg. 253)*

HCM #233
(Site of) SUNSET PLAZA APARTMENTS
1220 Sunset Plaza Drive, Hollywood. Designed by Paul R. Williams in the Georgian Revival taste, the apartments were a rare example of his work in multi-family housing and exhibited many features of his luxurious single-family residences (demolished July 1987).
Declared: 10/9/1980 *(pg. 370)*

HCM #234
(Site of) TAFT HOUSE
7777 West Sunset Boulevard, Hollywood (original location on Hollywood Boulevard). This Victorian farmhouse was moved in 1919. It was destroyed by fire in June of 1982.
Declared: 11/3/1980 *(pg. 126)*

HCM #235
BOLLMAN HOUSE
1530 North Ogden Drive, Hollywood. Built in 1922 and designed by Lloyd Wright, it is a concrete block structure with reinforcing steel rods. The building incorporates Mayan architectural motifs.
Declared: 11/3/1980 *(pg. 129)*

HCM #236
SUNSET BOULEVARD BRIDGE
Crossing over Silver Lake Boulevard, Los Angeles. Constructed in 1934, it is noted for its Romanesque arches and detailing.
Declared: 4/9/1981 *(pg. 281)*

HCM #237
FIRST BAPTIST CHURCH OF LOS ANGELES
760 South Westmoreland Avenue, Los Angeles. The church was built in 1927 by the firm of Allison & Allison.
Declared: 4/9/1981 *(pg. 334)*

HCM #238
GRANADA BUILDINGS
672 South Lafayette Park Place, Los Angeles. Built in 1927 by owner/designer Franklin Harper, the Mediterranean Revival buildings are organized around a landscaped court-yard with open corridors and bridges that crisscross the upper level.
Declared: 4/9/1981 *(pg. 411)*

HCM #239
LA CASA DE LAS CAMPAÑAS
350 North June Street, Los Angeles. Built in 1928 for the Mead family, the 37-room mansion has a three-story clock tower housing four massive bells. Designed by Lester Scherer, it is an example of Spanish Colonial Revival architecture.
Declared: 4/9/1981 *(pg. 389)*

HCM #240
RESIDENCE
2703 South Hoover Street, Los Angeles. Built circa 1891 and designed by Bradbeer & Ferris, this is an excellent example of a Queen Anne house.
Declared: 4/9/1981 *(pg. 312)*

HCM #241
SUNSHINE MISSION
2600 South Hoover Street, Los Angeles. Built in 1892 by Los Angeles architect Sumner P. Hunt in the Queen Anne style, it became the Girls Collegiate Boarding School in 1915. In 1942 it was turned into a home for destitute women and girls.
Declared: 4/9/1981 *(pg. 343)*

HCM #242
MILLER & HERRIOTT TRACT HOUSE
1163 West 27th Street, Los Angeles. Built in 1890, it is considered the oldest surviving example of a tract house. This Eastlake-style residence is noted for its outstanding exterior architecture, its magnificent staircase and interiors graced with original fireplaces and tiles.
Declared: 4/9/1981 *(pg. 340)*

HCM #243
(Site of) GARDEN COURT APARTMENTS
7021 Hollywood Boulevard, Hollywood. Designed by Frank L. Meline in the Classical style, the building opened with great fanfare in December 1919 and was to become one of Hollywood's largest and most prestigious apartment houses of the 1920s and 1930s (demolished 1984).
Declared: 4/28/1981 *(pg. 129)*

HCM #244
RESIDENCE
1866 West 14th Street, Los Angeles. Built in 1906 by lumberman Andrew Beyrle, the residence is noted for its fine Craftsman details.
Declared: 4/30/1981 *(pg. 335)*

HCM #245
LINCOLN AVENUE CHURCH BUILDING
Heritage Square, 3800 Homer Street, Los Angeles (original location at 732 North Orange Grove Boulevard, Pasadena). Built in 1897 and designed by architect George W. Kramer, the church is noted for its distinguishing Carpenter Gothic features with Queen Anne and Neoclassical influences. The church was relocated in 1981.
Declared: 6/4/1981 *(pg. 178)*

HCM #246
RESIDENCE
1443 North Martel Avenue, Los Angeles. Completed in 1913, this residence is an outstanding example of the California Bungalow style.
Declared:11/25/1981 *(pg. 128)*

HCM #247
FREEMAN HOUSE
1962 Glencoe Way, Los Angeles. Built in 1924, this is one of five L.A. houses by Frank Lloyd Wright. It is constructed of concrete block with Mayan influence.
Declared:11/25/1981 *(pg. 130)*

HCM #248
FIRST UNITED METHODIST CHURCH OF HOLLYWOOD
6817 Franklin Avenue, Hollywood. Designed by architect Thomas P. Barber, it has a steel-framed sanctuary made of concrete walls with a ceiling of open hammer-beam construction, a copy of the ceiling in London's Westminster Hall.
Declared:12/4/1981 *(pg. 131)*

36

HCM #249
POWDER MAGAZINE, CAMP DRUM
1001 Eubank Avenue and 561 East Opp Street, Wilmington. Built in 1862, the 20-by-20-foot brick and stone powder magazine served Camp Drum during the Civil War (See HCM #21).
Declared: 8/10/1982 *(pg. 264)*

HCM #250
EBELL OF LOS ANGELES
4400 Wilshire Boulevard, Los Angeles. Designed by Silas R. Burns and Sumner P. Hunt, the cornerstone of this Spanish Colonial Revival building was laid on February 28, 1927.
Declared: 8/25/1982 *(pg. 403)*

HCM #251
JUAREZ THEATER (formerly Warner Grand Theater)
478 West 6th Street, San Pedro. Built in 1931 by B. Marcus Priteca, this Art Deco theater retains original murals and furnishings. Recently restored as the Warner Grand Theatre, it is the only remaining movie palace of the three Priteca designed in San Pedro, Beverly Hills and Huntington Park.
Declared: 8/25/1982 *(pg. 269)*

HCM #252
HARBOR VIEW HOUSE
921 Beacon Street, San Pedro. This five-story Spanish Colonial Revival structure was dedicated on September 2, 1926 to serve as a recreational center for servicemen.
Declared: 8/25/1982 *(pg. 266)*

HCM #253
MULLER HOUSE
1542 Beacon Street, San Pedro (original location on Nob Hill; relocated to 575 19th Street circa 1911). Built circa 1899, this Colonial Revival structure contains leaded glass, detailed carving and wood paneling. It was moved to its present site in 1985. Open to the public.
Declared: 8/25/1982 *(pg. 270)*

HCM #254
MARYMOUNT HIGH SCHOOL (main administration building, chapel and auditorium)
10643 Sunset Boulevard, Los Angeles. Designed by Ross Montgomery and dedicated on February 2, 1932, the architecture is Spanish Colonial Revival with Mission style elements. The tile work, wrought iron, frescoes and stained glass are all exquisitely detailed.
Declared: 9/28/1982 *(pg. 352)*

HCM #255
THE ORIGINAL PANTRY
877 South Figueroa Street, Los Angeles. Opened for business in 1924, this restaurant consisted of one room with a fifteen-stool counter, a small grill, a hot plate and a sink. With the slogan "Never Closed—Never Without a Customer," it has grown in both size and reputation.
Declared:10/5/1982 *(pg. 39)*

HCM #256
MACK SENNETT STUDIOS
1712 Glendale Boulevard, Los Angeles. Built in 1912, this structure was one of the first motion picture studios in Los Angeles. The buildings date from the days when Sennett was recognized as the major producer of comedies in the business. Declared:11/5/1982 *(pg. 97)*

HCM #257
RESIDENCE
817 North Glendale Boulevard, Los Angeles. Built in 1937 and designed by John Victor Macka, this Mediterranean and Spanish Colonial residence has a view of Echo Park Lake. Declared:11/5/1982 *(pg. 98)*

HCM #258
FITZGERALD HOUSE
3115 West Adams Boulevard, Los Angeles. Constructed in 1903 in an Italian Gothic style, it was designed for J. T. Fitzgerald by Joseph Cather Newsom. Declared:11/5/1982 *(pg. 330)*

HCM #259
LOYOLA THEATER
8610 South Sepulveda Boulevard, Los Angeles. Built in 1948, this distinctive Baroque Moderne structure was designed by Clarence J. Smale. Its etched-glass doors, ticket booth and interior murals are unique. Declared:12/17/1982 *(pg. 20)*

HCM #260
EDWARDS HOUSE
5642 Holly Oak Drive, Hollywood Hills. Built in 1936 and designed by Gregory Ain in the International Style, it was named "House of the Year" in *House Beautiful* in 1938 and listed as one of the best small houses in America in the *Architectural Forum* in 1940. The residence features a trellised garden off the two bedrooms, leading around the corner to a small swimming pool. Declared: 5/17/1983 *(pg. 131)*

HCM #261
LINCOLN HEIGHTS BRANCH LIBRARY
2530 Workman Street, Lincoln Heights. Constructed in 1916 and designed by Hibbard & Cody, this Italian Renaissance building of brick and stucco is one of the few remaining Carnegie-funded libraries in the area. Declared: 6/3/1983 *(pg. 115)*

HCM #262
RESIDENCE
2700 Eagle Street, Boyle Heights. Built in 1890, this wood structure is an excellent example of the Queen Anne style. Major architectural features include a corner tower with an onion cap, a pitched roof and a raised offset entrance. Declared: 6/3/1983 *(pg. 167)*

HCM #263
VILLA RAFAEL
2123 Parkside Avenue, Los Angeles. The original portion of this house was built in 1904. In 1923 the property was acquired by Giovanni and Tranquilla Vai and modified in 1929 with J.A. Wilson as architect. It has a Spanish Colonial Revival exterior with an Italian Renaissance interior. Declared: 6/3/1983 *(pg. 107)*

HCM #264
VERMONT SQUARE BRANCH LIBRARY
1201 West 48th Street, Los Angeles. Opened in March 1913, it was the first permanent branch library building and the first of six Carnegie-funded buildings erected in Los Angeles. Designed by Sumner P. Hunt and Silas R. Burns, it is an example of Beaux Arts architecture with Prairie style and Italian Renaissance tendencies, set in a lovely park. Declared: 6/7/1983 *(pg. 38)*

HCM #265
BRIDGE
4th and Lorena Streets, Boyle Heights. Constructed in 1928 by the City of Los Angeles's Bureau of Engineering, it is one of a few remaining catenary arch bridges in the city. Declared: 6/7/1983 *(pg. 107)*

HCM #266
COLLINS RESIDENCE
890-892 West Kensington Road, Los Angeles (original location on Whittier Boulevard). Built circa 1888, this residence is designed in the Eastlake style. It was relocated in 1987. The first assessed owner, Michael Collins, was responsible for bringing the Santa Fe Railroad into the city. Declared: 6/10/1983 *(pg. 98)*

HCM #267
PARK PLAZA HOTEL
(formerly Elks Club)
607 South Park View Street, Los Angeles. Constructed in 1925 and designed by Aleck Curlett and Claude Beelman, the twelve-story structure is described as Beaux Arts with Bertram Goodhue influences. Architectural details include statuary, entry columns, brackets and a bronze arched entry. Declared: 6/24/1983 *(pg. 408)*

HCM #268
LA FONDA RESTAURANT BUILDING
2501 Wilshire Boulevard, Los Angeles. This 1926 building is a stucco-over-brick structure designed in the Spanish Colonial Revival style by Morgan, Walls & Clements. Declared: 6/24/1983 *(pg. 395)*

HCM #269
MOUNT WASHINGTON CABLE CAR STATION
200 West Avenue 43, Mt. Washington. Opened May 24, 1909 and closed on January 9, 1919, the Mission Revival funicular railway station survives today in a slightly altered form as a private residence. It was designed by Fred R. Dorn. Declared: 6/28/1983 *(pg. 175)*

HCM #270
VENICE CANAL SYSTEM
Area bounded by Venice Boulevard and Washington Street, west of Abbot Kinney Boulevard, Venice. Created by Norman F. Marsh, the canals opened June 30, 1905 as part of a unique subdivision including Ballona Lagoon and all of the Sherman, Howland, Linnie, Carroll, Eastern and Grand Canals. Arched bridges spanned the channels and Abbot Kinney imported gondolas and gondoliers from Italy to further replicate the ambiance of Venetian canals. Declared: 7/15/1983 *(pg. 19)*

HCM #271
FARMERS AND MERCHANTS BANK BUILDING
401 South Main Street, Los Angeles. Constructed in 1904 by founder Isaias Hellman, the building was designed by Octavius Morgan and John Walls. The bank is noted for being an important financial institution in the early days of Los Angeles. Declared: 8/9/1983 *(pg. 39)*

HCM #272
PEET HOUSE
1139 South Harvard Boulevard, Los Angeles. Built circa 1889, the house is a well-preserved example of the modest, two-story version of the Victorian "plan book" dwelling, lacking much of the elaborate ornamentation characteristic of the period. Declared: 9/21/1983 *(pg. 296)*

HCM #273
DURFEE HOUSE
1007 West 24th Street, Los Angeles. Built circa 1885 for Richmond Durfee and his wife, it is a wood frame house ornamented in the Eastlake style. Declared: 1/4/1984 *(pg. 347)*

HCM #274
NORTHEAST POLICE STATION
6045 York Boulevard, Highland Park. Constructed in 1926 in a Renaissance Revival style, the station is the last remaining representative of a typical police station of the 1920s, a period of tremendous growth in Los Angeles history. Declared: 1/4/1984 *(pg. 165)*

HCM #275
HEINSBERGEN BUILDING
7415 Beverly Boulevard, Los Angeles. Built in 1927, it was designed by architect Claude Beelman for the workshop of muralist and interior designer Anthony B. Heinsbergen, who created murals for more than 700 theaters, including the Pantages, Wiltern, Los Angeles and Million Dollar Theaters. Declared: 1/17/1984 *(pg. 219)*

HCM #276
PACIFIC PALISADES BUSINESS BLOCK (formerly Santa Monica Land and Water Company Building)
15300-15318 Sunset Boulevard, Pacific Palisades. Completed in 1924, the building was designed by architect Clifton Nourse in the Spanish Colonial Revival style. Declared: 4/24/1984 *(pg. 380)*

HCM #277
HOLLYWOOD MASONIC TEMPLE
6840 Hollywood Boulevard, Hollywood. Designed by (John C.) Austin, Field & Frey in 1921, this structure is the only remaining fraternal or civic institution on Hollywood Boulevard. The building has a classical façade, with the main features being a series of six oversized Ionic columns, an ornamental parapet and a frieze inlaid with symbols of the Masonic order. Declared: 6/12/1984 *(pg. 130)*

HCM #278
TITLE GUARANTEE & TRUST COMPANY BUILDING (exterior only)
401-411 West 5th Street, Los Angeles. Completed in 1931, this building was designed by the architectural firm of John and Donald Parkinson. The design of the building combines elements of the French Zigzag Moderne style with more typical Art Deco detailing. It is a twelve-story, plus tower, steel-framed building, clad in buff-colored terra cotta. Declared: 7/11/1984 *(pg. 37)*

HCM #279
GREENACRES
(the Harold Lloyd Estate)
1040 Angelo Drive, Los Angeles. This 1928 Mediterranean and Italian Renaissance structure designed by Sumner Spaulding is significant for its architectural features. Lloyd was one of the most successful silent film stars.
Declared: 7/24/1984 *(pg. 355)*

HCM #280
CHAPMAN PARK STUDIO BUILDING
3501-3519 West 6th Street, Los Angeles. Designed by the firm of Morgan, Walls & Clements, construction was completed in February, 1929. The exterior of this shop and studio building is Mediterranean Revival with Churrigueresque detail. It is of brick-and-steel construction, faced on the exterior with plaster, cast stone and wrought iron.
Declared: 7/24/1984 *(pg. 412)*

HCM #281
CATHEDRAL HIGH SCHOOL
1253 Bishops Road, Los Angeles. Founded in September 1923 in Sacred Heart Parish, the school is said to be the oldest Catholic high school established by the Archdiocese of Los Angeles.
Declared: 8/7/1984 *(pg. 38)*

HCM #282
MASONIC TEMPLE
104 North Avenue 56, Highland Park. Designed by Elmore R. Jeffrey and built in 1923, this Renaissance Revival building was designed for both institutional and commercial use.
Declared: 8/29/1984 *(pg. 173)*

HCM #283
SOUTHWEST MUSEUM
234 Museum Drive, Mt. Washington. Constructed between 1912 and 1914, the building was designed by the firm of Sumner P. Hunt and Silas R. Burns. It is one of the first major examples of the transition from Mission Revival to Spanish Colonial Revival in Los Angeles. The 1920 lower entrance on Museum Drive is Pre-Columbian Revival and was designed by the firm of Allison & Allison. Founded in 1903 by Charles F. Lummis to preserve the knowledge and artifacts of the native peoples of the American Southwest, it is the first museum established in Los Angeles and the oldest privately-endowed museum in California devoted to Native American culture. Open to the public.
Declared: 8/29/1984 *(pg. 193)*

HCM #284
HIGHLAND PARK EBELL CLUB
131 South Avenue 57, Highland Park. Designed by Sumner P. Hunt and Silas R. Burns, the main building was dedicated on February 4, 1913. Sidney Clifton designed the annex in 1937.
Declared: 8/29/1984 *(pg. 179)*

HCM #285
C.E. TOBERMAN ESTATE
1847 Camino Palmero, Hollywood. Completed in 1924, Russell, Alpaugh & Dawson designed this 19-room villa for the prominent real estate developer C.E. Toberman. The estate consists of an elegant three-story Mediterranean and Spanish Colonial Revival main house with a guesthouse, pool house and tennis court.
Declared: 10/3/1984 *(pg. 132)*

HCM #286
MAYFLOWER HOTEL
535 South Grand Avenue, Los Angeles. This Moorish-influenced structure was designed in 1927 by local architect Charles F. Whittlesey.
Declared: 10/5/1984 *(pg. 40)*

HCM #287
YOAKUM HOUSE
140 South Avenue 59, Highland Park. Constructed by mostly volunteer labor between 1895 and 1915, this large Tudor Revival house was built for Father Finis Ewing Yoakum, the founder of a halfway house called Pisgah Home.
Declared: 1/18/1985 *(pg. 172)*

HCM #288
BARCLAY HOTEL
(formerly Van Nuys Hotel)
103 West 4th Street, Los Angeles. Designed in 1896 by Octavius Morgan and J.A. Walls in the Beaux Arts style, it was the first Los Angeles hotel to provide a telephone in every room and have electricity throughout. The developer was Isaac Newton Van Nuys, a leading Los Angeles financier and founder of the community of Van Nuys.
Declared: 2/1/1985 *(pg. 42)*

HCM #289
FIRE STATION No. 30
1401 South Central Avenue, Los Angeles. Built in 1942 and designed by architect James Backus, it was the city's first fire station to be manned exclusively by African Americans. It was segregated for 25 years.
Declared: 2/15/1985 *(pg. 42)*

HCM #290
LA REINA THEATER
14626 Ventura Boulevard, Sherman Oaks. Opened in 1938, the 875-seat theater was a Streamline Moderne structure designed by Los Angeles architect S. Charles Lee. In 1987 its interior was gutted for shops and its façade and marquee were preserved and incorporated into the La Reina Fashion Plaza.
Declared: 3/6/1985 *(pg. 238)*

HCM #291
HIGHLAND-CAMROSE BUNGALOW VILLAGE
2103-2111½ North Highland Avenue / 6819 Camrose Drive, Hollywood. Constructed between 1916 and 1923, the homes comprise a village of California Craftsman and Dutch Colonial Revival bungalows clustered on a hillside. The complex was built during the prime period of Hollywood's development.
Declared: 4/23/1985 *(pg. 132)*

HCM #292
OLD EAGLE ROCK BRANCH LIBRARY
2225 Colorado Boulevard, Eagle Rock. Originally constructed in 1914, it was remodeled in 1927 by architects Henry C. Newton and Robert D. Murray. They incorporated a Spanish ecclesiastical scheme into the building.
Declared: 6/18/1985 *(pg. 165)*

HCM #293
THE MAGNOLIA
13242 Magnolia Boulevard, Sherman Oaks. Built in the late 1920s, this Spanish Colonial residence includes a detached garage and chauffeur's quarters.
Declared: 6/18/1985 *(pg. 250)*

HCM #294
EASTERN-COLUMBIA BUILDING
849 South Broadway, Los Angeles. Designed by Claude Beelman in 1930, this building is the finest remaining example in downtown Los Angeles of French Zigzag Moderne design, typical of the Art Deco period. The thirteen-story structure has a strong verticality due to deeply recessed bands of paired metal-sash casement windows set between fluted vertical piers.
Declared: 6/28/1985 *(pg. 41)*

HCM #295
A.E. KELLY RESIDENCE
1140 West Adams Boulevard, Los Angeles. Constructed in the 1890s, this house was built in the Queen Anne style. The first floor exterior walls are composed of wood clapboard siding and the second floor walls of fish-scale shingles.
Declared: 7/12/1985 *(pg. 320)*

HCM #296
JOHN C. HARRISON HOUSE
1160 West 27th Street, Los Angeles. Built circa 1891 for John Cleves Short Harrison, a retired Indiana businessman, it is an example of the Queen Anne style. It is the largest surviving house in the Miller & Herriott Tract.
Declared: 7/12/1985 *(pg. 343)*

HCM #297
WEST ADAMS GARDENS
1158-1176 West Adams Boulevard, Los Angeles. Constructed in 1920, these seven residential buildings have stucco exterior walls with exposed half-timber framing and are designed in a manner influenced by the Tudor Revival style.
Declared: 8/13/1985 *(pg. 327)*

HCM #298
CROCKER BANK BUILDING
273 South Western Avenue, Los Angeles. The structure was designed in 1931 by Arthur E. Harvey and is one of the few remaining black-and-gold Art Deco buildings in Los Angeles. The building originally housed a clothing store.
Declared: 9/20/1985 *(pg. 391)*

HCM #299
EMBASSY AUDITORIUM AND HOTEL
851 South Grand Avenue, Los Angeles. Work on the Embassy Hotel began in 1913 by architect Thornton Fitzhugh. This nine-story, steel-and-concrete edifice in the Beaux Arts style has a majestic, four-story Baroque dome. The 1500-seat auditorium is reminiscent of old European concert halls, compact and finely detailed.
Declared: 10/4/1985 *(pg. 41)*

HCM #300
CASA CAMINO REAL
1828 South Oak Street, Los Angeles. Built in 1924 and designed by the firm of Morgan, Walls & Clements, the exterior is Beaux Arts with Art Deco and Spanish-influenced windows.
Declared: 10/29/1985 *(pg. 45)*

HCM #301
ARZNER/MORGAN RESIDENCE
2249 Mountain Oak Drive, Los Angeles. Designed by architect W.C. Tanner in 1931, the Arzner/Morgan residence resembles a Grecian villa. It was once the residence of Dorothy Arzner, one of the few female directors who worked in early Hollywood, and Marian Morgan, the talented avant-garde *danseuse*.
Declared: 2/28/1986 *(pg. 154)*

HCM #302
AMELIA EARHART / NORTH HOLLYWOOD BRANCH LIBRARY
5211 North Tujunga Avenue, North Hollywood. Built in 1929, it was designed by Lewis Eugene Weston and his son Lewis Eugene Weston, Jr. in the Spanish Colonial Revival style. Declared: 6/27/1986 *(pg. 256)*

HCM #303
JOHN C. FREMONT BRANCH LIBRARY
6121 Melrose Avenue, Los Angeles. Designed by Merl Lee Barker in 1927, the library is an example of Mediterranean architecture. Declared: 6/27/1986 *(pg. 389)*

HCM #304
MALABAR BRANCH LIBRARY
2801 East Wabash Avenue, Los Angeles. Designed in 1927 by William Lee Woolett, it is reminiscent of rural Latin American architecture. Declared: 6/27/1986 *(pg. 111)*

HCM #305
JOHN MUIR BRANCH LIBRARY
1005 West 64th Street, Los Angeles. Built in 1930 and designed by local architect Henry F. Withey, the building is Italian Renaissance in style. Declared: 6/27/1986 *(pg. 45)*

HCM #306
(Site of) ORIGINAL VERNON BRANCH LIBRARY
4504 South Central Avenue, Los Angeles. The building housed a large and significant special collection of books on African American history. It was damaged beyond repair in the 1971 Sylmar earthquake. Declared: 6/27/1986 *(pg. 43)*

HCM #307
WASHINGTON IRVING BRANCH LIBRARY
1803 South Arlington Avenue, Los Angeles. Built in 1926 and designed by Allison & Allison, the library is an excellent example of Lombardic Romanesque Revival architecture. Declared: 6/27/1986 *(pg. 315)*

HCM #308
WILMINGTON BRANCH LIBRARY
309 West Opp Street, Wilmington. Constructed in 1927, the Spanish Colonial Revival building was designed by Sylvanus Marston, Garrett Van Pelt and Edgar Maybury. Declared: 6/27/1986 *(pg. 271)*

HCM #309
EL ROYALE APARTMENTS
450 North Rossmore Avenue, Los Angeles. Designed by William Douglas Lee circa 1920, this twelve-story apartment building has elements of Spanish and French Renaissance details. Declared: 9/2/1986 *(pg. 388)*

HCM #310
FIRE STATION No. 29
158 South Western Avenue, Los Angeles. Completed in 1913 and designed by architect J.J. Backus, the brick building is Italian Renaissance in style. Declared: 10/1/1986 *(pg. 398)*

HCM #311
LOS ALTOS APARTMENTS
4121 Wilshire Boulevard, Los Angeles. Designed by Edward B. Rust, construction began in 1925. It is an elegant example of Spanish Revival with Italianate ornamentation. Declared: 10/17/1986 *(pg. 388)*

HCM #312
JAPANESE UNION CHURCH OF LOS ANGELES
(exterior only)
120 North San Pedro Street, Los Angeles. Designed by H.M. Patterson and dedicated in 1923, it was the first purpose-built house of worship in Los Angeles for Protestant Japanese Americans. The structure also served as a community center. Declared:10/24/1986 *(pg. 43)*

HCM #313
LOS ANGELES HOMPA HONGWANJI BUDDHIST TEMPLE
(exterior and sanctuary)
355-369 East 1st Street / 109-119 North Central Avenue, Los Angeles. Constructed 1924-1925 and designed by Edgar Cline, it was one of the first religious structures serving Asian Americans in Los Angeles. The building has three sections, each architecturally and historically distinct from each other. Today it is the Japanese American National Museum. Open to the public. Declared:10/24/1986 *(pg. 47)*

HCM #314
CAHUENGA BRANCH LIBRARY
4591 West Santa Monica Boulevard, Los Angeles. Designed by architect Clarence H. Russell, this Carnegie-funded library was completed in 1916. Declared:10/24/1986 *(pg. 132)*

HCM #315
VILLA CARLOTTA
5959 Franklin Avenue, Hollywood. Designed by architect Arthur E. Harvey in 1926, this Churrigueresque structure was constructed with an elaborate system of soundproofing, a water filtration system, a central refrigeration system and a ventilation system that changes air in each apartment every five minutes. Declared:10/28/1986 *(pg. 134)*

HCM #316
WILLIAM STROMBERG CLOCK
6439 Hollywood Boulevard, Hollywood. A landmark since 1927, the clock is associated with one of the boulevard's oldest retailers. Declared: 1/7/1987 *(pg. 126)*

HCM #317
YOUNG APARTMENTS
1621 South Grand Avenue, Los Angeles. Constructed in 1921 and designed by architect Robert Brown Young, the building is a Classical Revival design. Declared: 1/7/1987 *(pg. 44)*

HCM #318
HOLMBY HOUSE
1221-1223 Holmby Avenue, Los Angeles. Built in the late 1920s, the Holmby House is a fine example of the Mediterranean style. Declared: 2/13/1987 *(pg. 377)*

HCM #319
THE GROVE
10669-10683 Santa Monica Boulevard, Westwood (original location at 10569 and 10571 Santa Monica Boulevard). One of the few remaining courtyard dwellings designed by architect Allen Siple, with additional lofts by Edla Muir, these French Revival structures are evidence of the meticulousness the Janss Development Company took in creating Westwood. In 1989 The Grove was relocated, slightly reconfigured and rehabilitated for use as shops for tenants of adjacent buildings. Declared: 3/11/1987 *(pg. 353)*

HCM #320
LANDFAIR APARTMENTS
10940-10954 Ophir Drive, Westwood. Built in 1937, this International Style structure was designed by Richard Neutra. Declared: 5/20/1987 *(pg. 364)*

HCM #321
EASTLAKE INN
1442 Kellam Avenue, Los Angeles. This is a circa 1887 Victorian structure. Declared: 5/20/1987 *(pg. 98)*

HCM #322
FLETCHER DRIVE BRIDGE
Fletcher Drive between Larga Avenue and Crystal Street, Los Angeles. Designed by the Bureau of Engineering of the City of Los Angeles and completed in 1928, this bridge is built of reinforced concrete. Declared: 7/21/1987 *(pg. 281)*

HCM #323
(Site of) CHURCH OF THE OPEN DOOR
550 South Hope Street, Los Angeles. Completed in 1915, this Italian Renaissance design by Walker & Vawter was built with two thirteen-story towers surrounding a large auditorium (demolished 1988). Declared: 7/28/1987 *(pg. 47)*

HCM #324
THE LINDBROOK
10800-10808 Lindbrook Drive, Westwood. Built in 1935, this is an example of the Mediterranean courtyard apartment complexes associated with Westwood Village. Declared: 8/14/1987 *(pg. 372)*

HCM #325
SHULMAN HOUSE
7875 Woodrow Wilson Drive, Hollywood Hills. Built in 1950 by local architect Raphael Soriano, this is his only residence in Los Angeles in its original state. The house was built for noted architectural photographer Julius Shulman, many of whose photographs appear in this guide. Declared: 8/26/1987 *(pg. 352)*

HCM #326
(Site of) McKINLEY MANSION
310 South Lafayette Park Place, Los Angeles. Built in 1917 and designed by Sumner P. Hunt and Silas R. Burns, this generously proportioned building was originally surrounded by a large Classical garden. It was gutted by fire and demolished in 1994. Declared: 9/9/1987 *(pg. 392)*

HCM #327
THOMAS POTTER RESIDENCE
1135 South Alvarado Street, Los Angeles. In 1906 the firm of Hudson & Munsell was commissioned to design this ten-room residence. Its brick-and-stucco structure displays many elements associated with the Tudor Revival style.
Declared: 9/22/1987 *(pg. 415)*

HCM #328
AUGUST WINSTEL RESIDENCE
1147 South Alvarado Street, Los Angeles. Built in 1907, the structure is the work of local architect John Paul Krempel.
Declared: 9/22/1987 *(pg. 412)*

HCM #329
CHATEAU ELYSEE
5930 Franklin Avenue, Hollywood. Built as a residential hotel in 1928 by Eleanor Ince, the Chateau Revival building was designed by Arthur E. Harvey.
Declared: 9/23/1987 *(pg. 135)*

HCM #330
ROSEDALE CEMETERY
1831 West Washington Boulevard, Los Angeles. Opened in 1884, it is one of the earliest cemeteries in Los Angeles still in operation and was the first in the West to build and operate a crematorium. Its concentration of pioneer family burial sites is unusual, and the examples of funerary architecture are outstanding.
Declared:12/1/1987 *(pg. 321)*

HCM #331
PACIFIC BELL BUILDING
2755 West 15th Street, Los Angeles. Built circa 1922, this Spanish Mission style garage features Churrigueresque detail.
Declared:12/8/1987 *(pg. 307)*

HCM #332
WILSHIRE TOWER
5514 Wilshire Boulevard, Los Angeles. In the first building to meet the city's height limit on Wilshire Boulevard's Miracle Mile, architect Gilbert Stanley Underwood combined a slender tower with a larger horizontal base. The style is unusual because of its combination of French Zigzag and Streamline Moderne elements.
Declared:12/8/1987 *(pg. 221)*

HCM #333
GRIER-MUSSER HOUSE
403 South Bonnie Brae Street, Los Angeles. Built in 1898 by Jonathan H. Hill, this is a rectangular Queen Anne and Colonial Revival wood structure. Open to the public.
Declared:12/18/1987 *(pg. 390)*

HCM #334
SECURITY TRUST & SAVINGS BUILDING
6381-6385 Hollywood Boulevard, Hollywood. One of the first high-rise (seven stories) buildings on Hollywood Boulevard, it was designed by the firm of Parkinson & Parkinson in 1921 in the Beaux Arts and Italian Renaissance Revival styles.
Declared:12/18/1987 *(pg. 134)*

HCM #335
HENRY J. REUMAN RESIDENCE
925 West 23rd Street, Los Angeles. This residence, designed by August Wackerbarth circa 1896, is a wood structure that illustrates a transition between Colonial Revival and Queen Anne architecture.
Declared:12/18/1987 *(pg. 344)*

HCM #336
HOLLYWOOD-WESTERN BUILDING
5500-5510 Hollywood Boulevard, Los Angeles. Constructed in 1928 from a design by architect S. Charles Lee, this Art Deco building housed the famed Central Casting offices for many years.
Declared: 1/6/1988 *(pg. 156)*

HCM #337
ENGINE COMPANY No. 56
2838 Rowena Avenue, Los Angeles. Built in 1924, this is one of the few unaltered Mediterranean Bungalow engine houses built in Los Angeles in the 1920s. Its design combines elements of the Spanish Colonial Revival and Classical Revival styles.
Declared: 1/12/1988 *(pg. 282)*

HCM #338
DRAKE HOUSE
220 South Avenue 60, Highland Park. Built in 1894, this structure is a Midwestern-style farmhouse with Eastlake influences and 20th century additions.
Declared: 1/26/1988 *(pg. 187)*

HCM #339
SANTA FE ARROYO SECO RAILROAD BRIDGE
162 South Avenue 61 at 110 Freeway, Highland Park. Constructed in 1896, it is the highest railroad bridge in Los Angeles County and possibly the oldest one in use. Over 700 feet long and 100 feet above the Pasadena Freeway, it is made of steel on concrete footings originally that supported a single-track railroad line. In September 1996 it was rededicated after being renovated by the Metropolitan Transportation Authority and converted to a double-track rail line for use as a part of the Los Angeles-to-Pasadena Gold Line.
Declared: 1/22/1988 *(pg. 181)*

HCM #340
STANDARD OIL BUILDING
605 West Olympic Boulevard, Los Angeles. This building was designed by architect George W. Kelham in 1928 in the Beaux Arts style.
Declared: 1/26/1988 *(pg. 46)*

HCM #341
FIRST AFRICAN METHODIST EPISCOPAL ZION CATHEDRAL AND COMMUNITY CENTER
1449 West Adams Boulevard, Los Angeles. Built in 1930 for the West Adams Presbyterian Church, this complex of buildings was the work of architects H.M. Patterson and George W. Kelham. The cathedral is an example of Romanesque Revival style and housed one of the early African American congregations in Los Angeles.
Declared: 1/22/1988 *(pg. 345)*

HCM #342
MASONIC TEMPLE
227 North Avalon Boulevard, Wilmington. Built in 1882, this structure is the oldest known non-residential structure still standing in Wilmington. In 1912, the building was raised, set back and repaired when Canal Street (now Avalon Boulevard) was widened. It is a fine example of Renaissance Revival architecture with many of its original details in place.
Declared: 1/22/1988 *(pg. 270)*

HCM #343
AVOCADO TREES
4400 Block of Avocado Street, Los Angeles. The trees have been growing for 100 years. Eight of the original twenty-five trees remain.
Declared: 1/22/1988 *(pg. 283)*

HCM #344
INSTITUTE OF MUSICAL ART (formerly C.B.A. Studios)
3210 West 54th Street, Los Angeles. C.B.A. (Clark Brown Audio) Studios had its origin in 1970 when Ray G. Clark and Oliver P. Brown, both space engineers, designed and built recording facilities at this location. C.B.A. has played an important role in African American music recording history.
Declared: 2/23/1988 *(pg. 18)*

HCM #345
HARRIS NEWMARK BUILDING
127 East 9th Street, Los Angeles. Designed in 1926 by Curlett & Beelman for the Newmark family, this commercial twelve-story building is characterized by the popular Renaissance Revival style. Harris Newmark, who died in 1916, was an important early Los Angeles historian.
Declared: 2/23/1988 *(pg. 49)*

HCM #346
COAST FEDERAL SAVINGS BUILDING
315 West 9th Street, Los Angeles. Designed by the firm of Morgan, Walls & Clements, this twelve-story, U-shaped structure was built in 1926. The exterior exemplifies Period Revival, a style popular for commercial structures of the time.
Declared: 3/11/1988 *(pg. 51)*

HCM #347
ONE BUNKER HILL BUILDING (formerly Southern California Edison Building)
601 West 5th Street, Los Angeles. Built between 1930-1934 and designed by Allison & Allison, it was one of the first all-electric buildings in the western United States and one of the first earthquake-proof buildings in Los Angeles. In its time, this Art Deco, fourteen-story, steel-frame building was at the forefront of engineering technology.
Declared: 3/25/1988 *(pg. 48)*

HCM #348
FIRE STATION No. 28
644 South Figueroa Street, Los Angeles. This structure was built in 1912 from designs by John P. Krempel and Walter Erekes.
Declared: 3/29/1988 *(pg. 53)*

HCM #349
FIRE STATION No. 18
2616 South Hobart Boulevard, Los Angeles. This Mission Revival brick building was erected between 1904 and 1906 and designed by John Parkinson. It is one of the few fire stations remaining from the days of horse-drawn vehicles.
Declared: 3/29/1988 *(pg. 293)*

HCM #350
ECUNG-IBBETSON HOUSE AND MORETON BAY FIG TREE
1190 West Adams Boulevard, Los Angeles. Built in 1899 for a prominent real estate man, this residence features an eclectic combination of Romanesque and Victorian styles. Declared: 3/29/1988 *(pg. 308)*

HCM #351
STRATHMORE APARTMENTS
11005-11013½ Strathmore Drive, Los Angeles. Built in 1937 by Richard Neutra, these apartments are examples of International Style. Declared: 4/8/1988 *(pg. 370)*

HCM #352
LOS ANGELES NURSES' CLUB
245 South Lucas Avenue, Los Angeles. Built in 1923 to designs by architect John Frauenfelder, this Classical Revival building is an important example of institutional housing for nurses. Declared: 4/8/1988 *(pg. 46)*

HCM #353
MONTEREY APARTMENTS
4600 Los Feliz Boulevard, Los Angeles. Attributed to architect C.K. Smithley, these Mediterranean style apartments were constructed in 1925. Declared: 5/11/1988 *(pg. 285)*

HCM #354
GIANNINI/ BANK OF AMERICA
649 South Olive Street, Los Angeles. Built in 1922 for the Bank of Italy (now Bank of America), from a design by Morgan, Walls & Clements, this Renaissance Revival building includes monumental Corinthian columns, decorative ironwork and rusticated stone. Declared: 4/26/1988 *(pg. 54)*

HCM #355
ROOSEVELT BUILDING
727 West 7th Street, Los Angeles. Designed in 1923 by Curlett & Beelman, this twelve-story building is representative of Beaux Arts and Renaissance Revival styles. It features monumental arches on the 7th Street façade. Declared: 4/26/1988 *(pg. 55)*

HCM #356
BARKER BROTHERS BUILDING
818 West 7th Street, Los Angeles. This building was constructed in 1925 to house the principal store of Southern California's largest home furnishings company. Designed by Curlett & Beelman, it is a fine example of Beaux Arts and Renaissance Revival styles. Declared: 4/26/1988 *(pg. 51)*

HCM #357
BOSTON STORE/ J.W. ROBINSON'S
600 West 7th Street, Los Angeles. Constructed in 1915 for a major Los Angeles department store, it was completely remodeled in 1934 to designs by Allison & Allison. Declared: 4/26/1988 *(pg. 49)*

HCM #358
BROCK JEWELERS/ CLIFTON'S
513 West 7th Street, Los Angeles. This four-story building was constructed in 1922 for a prominent Los Angeles manufacturing jeweler from a design by Dodd & Richards. It now houses Clifton's Cafeteria and includes many of the original interior appointments. Declared: 4/15/1988 *(pg. 55)*

HCM #359
CONGREGATION TALMUD TORAH
247 North Breed Street, Boyle Heights. Architects A.M. Edelman & Leo W. Barnett designed the building with a Renaissance exterior and an interior reminiscent of Eastern European synagogues. It was dedicated in 1923. Declared: 6/7/1988 *(pg. 113)*

HCM #360
BRATSKELLER/EGYPTIAN THEATRE
1142-1154 Westwood Boulevard, Westwood. This structure, designed in 1929 by Russell Collins, conformed to the Mediterranean architectural guidelines for Westwood Village set up by the Janss Corporation. Originally opened as a Ralphs grocery store, it has been adapted to function as a restaurant and movie theater. Declared: 6/21/1988 *(pg. 371)*

HCM #361
FOX BRUIN THEATRE
926-950 Broxton Avenue, Westwood. It was designed by theater architect S. Charles Lee in 1937. The Streamline Moderne marquee is the principal visual feature of the façade. Declared: 6/21/1988 *(pg. 383)*

HCM #362
FOX VILLAGE THEATRE
945 Broxton Avenue, Westwood. Completed in 1931, this theater was the first entertainment facility in Westwood Village. Designed by P.P. Lewis in Spanish Classical Revival style for the Janss Corporation, the exterior remains virtually unchanged and still retains its original neon sign. Declared: 6/21/1988 *(pg. 379)*

HCM #363
GAYLEY TERRACE
*959 Gayley Avenue,
Westwood*. Completed in
1940 and designed by
Laurence B. Clapp, this
white-stucco Spanish
Colonial Revival apartment
building accommodates the
slope of the lot in the manner of a Mediterranean hill
town.
Declared: 6/21/1988 *(pg. 383)*

HCM #364
**JANSS INVESTMENT
COMPANY BUILDING**
*1045-1099 Westwood
Boulevard, Westwood*. Built
in 1929, this building was
designed in the Classical
style by Allison & Allison for
the Janss Corporation, cre-
ators of Westwood Village,
to use as their offices. The
building's dome is a visual
highlight, which distinguish-
es it from its surroundings.
Declared: 6/21/1988 *(pg. 365)*

HCM #365
KELTON APARTMENTS
*644 Kelton Avenue,
Westwood*. Built in 1941, it
was designed by Richard
Neutra in the International
Style.
Declared: 6/21/1988 *(pg. 355)*

HCM #366
**LATTER HOUSE AND
ARROYO STONE WALL**
*141 South Avenue 57,
Highland Park*. This unique
example of the 19th-century
design known as
Midwestern Gothic appears
to have been built in the
late 1880s, with subsequent
additions in the 1950s.
Declared: 6/21/1988 *(pg. 209)*

HCM #367
SHEETS APARTMENTS
*10901-10919 Strathmore
Drive, Westwood*. Designed
by John Lautner in 1949, it
is one of the most futuristic
structures in the North
Village.
Declared: 6/21/1988 *(pg. 378)*

HCM #368
ELKAY APARTMENTS
*638 Kelton Avenue,
Westwood*. Built in 1948,
the apartments are the last
structures by architect
Richard Neutra to be com-
pleted in the North Village.
Declared: 6/21/1988 *(pg. 359)*

HCM #369
**JOHNSON HOUSE AND
ARROYO STONE WALL**
*4985 Sycamore Terrace,
Highland Park*. The Johnson
House was the first of three
Craftsman houses that were
designed by Meyer &
Holler's Milwaukee Building
Company to be on "The
Terrace." It was built in 1911
and the billiard room was
added in 1912.
Declared: 7/15/1988 *(pg. 194)*

HCM #370
**HERIVEL HOUSE AND
ARROYO STONE WALL**
*4979 Sycamore Terrace,
Highland Park*. In 1912, the
Herivel House was construct-
ed in the Craftsman style for
John Johnson. It was
designed by Meyer &
Holler's Milwaukee Building
Company and constructed
by the California Real Estate
& Building Company.
Declared: 7/15/1988 *(pg. 200)*

HCM #371
**TUSTIN HOUSE AND
ARROYO STONE WALL**
*4973 Sycamore Terrace,
Highland Park*. Built in 1912
in the Craftsman style by
Meyer & Holler's Milwaukee
Building Company, this
house was built for Mary
Tustin, widow of the
founder of Tustin,
California.
Declared: 7/15/1988 *(pg. 192)*

HCM #372
**MARY P. FIELD HOUSE AND
ARROYO STONE WALL**
*4967 Sycamore Terrace,
Highland Park*. Built in 1903
for Mary Field, this house is
an example of a Craftsman
bungalow with chalet
touches.
Declared: 7/15/1988 *(pg. 204)*

HCM #373
**ARROYO STONE HOUSE
AND ARROYO STONE WALL**
*4939 Sycamore Terrace,
Highland Park*. Also known
as the Beach-Johnson
House, this structure was
built in 1900 with stone
from the Arroyo Seco.
Declared: 7/15/1988 *(pg. 171)*

HCM #374
G.W.E. GRIFFITH HOUSE
*5915 Echo Street, Highland
Park* (original location at
110 South Avenue 58). Built
in 1903, it was moved in
1914 to its present address.
It is believed to have been
designed by architect Fred
R. Dorn, who designed several other homes for Griffith
during the same period. The
Colonial Revival structure
has two balconies with
Moorish influences.
Declared: 7/15/1988 *(pg. 177)*

HCM #375
PUTNAM HOUSE
5944 Hayes Avenue,
Highland Park. Constructed
in 1903, this house is a mix
of Craftsman and Colonial
Revival styles. The architect,
George H. Wyman, is known
for the Bradbury Building
(HCM #6).
Declared: 7/15/1988 *(pg. 196)*

HCM #376
WILLIAM U. SMITH HOUSE
AND ARROYO STONE WALL
140 South Avenue 57,
Highland Park. The William
U. Smith House is owner-
built and patterned after his
former home in Pennsyl-
vania. The Greek Revival
bungalow was built in 1908.
Declared: 7/15/1988 *(pg. 190)*

HCM #377
OLLIE TRACT
179-199 South Avenue 57,
Highland Park. The Ollie
Tract has two homes (one is
a 1906 Craftsman by builder
John H. Scott), surrounded
by a park-like setting of
ancient oak trees and other
native trees and shrubs.
Declared: 7/15/1988 *(pg. 180)*

HCM #378
WHEELER-SMITH HOUSE
5684 Ash Street, Highland
Park. In 1897 Edgar
Wheeler, who was the Los
Angeles City Engineer, built
this house on his five-acre
property. The house,
designed by Howard &
Train, is Victorian in its
detailing but is transitional
in its Classical symmetry.
Declared: 7/15/1988 *(pg. 176)*

HCM #379
MORRELL HOUSE
215 North Avenue 53,
Highland Park. This house
was designed in 1906 for
organist John B. Morrell. It is
a Craftsman with many
interesting non-Craftsman
details, designed by Charles
E. Shattuck.
Declared: 7/15/1988 *(pg. 176)*

HCM #380
REEVES HOUSE
219 North Avenue 53,
Highland Park. Built in 1905,
this Colonial Revival house
was designed for a local
schoolteacher.
Declared: 7/15/1988 *(pg. 186)*

HCM #381
EAMES HOUSE, STUDIO
AND GROUNDS
(CASE STUDY HOUSE #8)
203 Chautauqua Boulevard,
Pacific Palisades. Designed
by Charles Eames between
1947 and 1949, it is a steel-
and-glass structure that utilizes industrial design.
Declared: 7/15/1988 *(pg. 356)*

HCM #382
FALCON STUDIOS
5524 Hollywood Boulevard,
Los Angeles. Built in the
1920s, this site hosted many
Hollywood performers, many
of whose signatures and
hand prints were once featured in the garden.
Declared: 7/26/1988 *(pg. 139)*

HCM #383
RESIDENCE
1203-1207 Kipling Avenue,
Eagle Rock. This Storybook-
style residence, playhouse
and studio designed by
architect H.A. Edwards, show
Craftsman overtones.
Declared: 8/5/1988 *(pg. 206)*

HCM #384
WATER AND POWER
BUILDING
2417 Daly Street, Lincoln
Heights. Remodeled to its
present condition by theater
architect S. Charles Lee, this
Art Deco building represents
the Department of Water
and Power's usage of the
Moderne style for its district
offices.
Declared: 8/5/1988 *(pg. 110)*

HCM #385
TITLE INSURANCE & TRUST
COMPANY BUILDING AND
ANNEX
419 (Annex) and 433
(Building) South Spring
Street, Los Angeles. The
complex of two buildings,
designed by architect John
Parkinson, is an example of
restrained French Zigzag
Moderne style. The main
lobby utilizes French Zigzag
and Art Deco motifs.
Declared: 8/5/1988 *(pg. 52)*

HCM #386
CHAPMAN PARK MARKET
BUILDING
3451 West 6th Street, Los
Angeles. Built in 1929, it was
one of the earliest auto-ori-
ented markets in the west-
ern United States. Designed
by architects Morgan, Walls
& Clements, it uses
Churrigueresque detailing.
Declared: 8/30/1988 *(pg. 50)*

HCM #387
GAS STATION
110 South Barrington
Avenue, Brentwood. This
station was built in 1939 in
Spanish Colonial style and
was designed by architect
Raymond A. Stockdale. The
most impressive design element is a two-story central
tower.
Declared: 9/2/1988 *(pg. 376)*

HCM #388
EDISON ELECTRIC COMPANY LOS ANGELES, No. 3 STEAM POWER PLANT
650 South Avenue 21, Lincoln Heights. Built in 1904, the No. 3 Plant was the largest of Edison's steam plants at that time. This brick-and-reinforced concrete building was designed by John Parkinson.
Declared:10/21/1988 *(pg. 80)*

HCM #389
C.M. CHURCH HOUSE
5907 Echo Street, Highland Park. Built in 1912, this Craftsman bungalow was designed by architect Henry J. Knauer. It is a good example of the use of river stone in a residence.
Declared:10/4/1988 *(pg. 207)*

HCM #390
JARDINETTE APARTMENTS
5128 Marathon Street, Los Angeles. Built in 1927, this is the earliest work in the United States by modernist Richard Neutra.
Declared:10/4/1988 *(pg. 142)*

HCM #391
CANFIELD-MORENO ESTATE
1923 Micheltorena Street, Silver Lake. In 1923, architect Robert D. Farquhar designed a 22-room Mediterranean country villa and detached cottages for Daisy Canfield Danziger. She lived there with her husband, actor Antonio Moreno. The site is also referred to as Danziger House and as Crestmount.
Declared:10/4/1988 *(pg. 284)*

HCM #392
TREEHAVEN, GUEST HOUSE AND GROUNDS
4211 Glenalbyn Drive, Mt. Washington. Built circa 1908, the main house is a large Craftsman residence constructed by owner/builder Charles E. Bent. The pavilion house was built as an art studio.
Declared:11/4/1988 *(pg. 169)*

HCM #393
WILES HOUSE
4224 Glenalbyn Drive, Mt. Washington. Designed and built by owner William Wilson in 1911, this Craftsman "Butterfly" bungalow is a rare design.
Declared:11/4/1988 *(pg. 198)*

HCM #394
ERNEST BENT/ FLORENCE BENT HALSTEAD HOUSE AND GROUNDS
4200 Glenalbyn Drive, Mt. Washington. The 1906 residence is a large Craftsman house.
Declared:11/4/1988 *(pg. 185)*

HCM #395
H. STANLEY BENT HOUSE, CARRIAGE HOUSE AND FRONT FOUNTAIN
4201 Glenalbyn Drive, Mt. Washington. Built circa 1912, the house and carriage house were designed by Mayberry & Parker. The grounds are a rare example of a Prairie-style estate.
Declared:11/4/1988 *(pg. 195)*

HCM #396
FEDERAL BANK BUILDING
2201 North Broadway, Lincoln Heights. Built circa 1910, this unusual Italian Renaissance building features a corner dome designed by architects Neher & Skilling.
Declared:11/23/1988 *(pg. 110)*

HCM #397
ROMAN GARDENS
2000 North Highland Avenue, Hollywood. Built in 1926 and designed by Walter S. Davis and F. Pierpont Davis, the design draws on Italian, Spanish and Moorish elements.
Declared:11/23/1988 *(pg. 136)*

HCM #398
PACIFIC MUTUAL BUILDING
523 West 6th Street, Los Angeles. The building incorporates three separate structures. The 1908 Beaux Arts unit, originally designed by John Parkinson and Edwin Bergstrom, was remodeled in 1937. The twelve-story building, designed by Dodd & Richards, was built in 1922. The third structure is a three-story parking garage added in 1926.
Declared:11/23/1988 *(pg. 52)*

HCM #399
BATES HOUSE
1415 Carroll Avenue, Los Angeles (original location at 1425 West Pico Boulevard; relocated to 725 South Bernal Avenue in 1921). Built in 1893, this Queen Anne residence was moved to its present location in 1988. Sunburst designs decorate the gables.
Declared:11/29/1988 *(pg. 99)*

HCM #400
SUN RISE COURT
5721-5729 Monte Vista Street, Highland Park. The court is a group of small bungalows in the Mission Revival style built in 1921 for Max and Lena Kogan and designed by Charles Conrad.
Declared:11/23/1988 *(pg. 188)*

HCM #401
FELIZ ADOBE
4730 Crystal Springs Drive, Griffith Park. Built circa 1853, the adobe was extensively remodeled in the 1920s.
Declared:11/30/1988 *(pg. 280)*

HCM #402
ASHLEY HOUSE
740-742 North Avenue 66, Garvanza. This Classical Revival residence was built by its owner, architect Frederick M. Ashley.
Declared:12/9/1988 *(pg. 191)*

HCM #403
HIGGINS/VERBECK/HIRSCH MANSION
637 South Lucerne Boulevard, Hancock Park (original location at 2619 Wilshire Boulevard). Built in 1902 and designed by John C. Austin, this late Queen Anne house with Romanesque detail was relocated in 1924 to its present site.
Declared:12/14/1988 *(pg. 410)*

HCM #404
(Site of) LOS ANGELES RAILWAY HURON SUBSTATION
2640 North Huron Street, Cypress Park. Built in 1906 from a design by engineer Edward S. Cobb, it is the second-oldest surviving substation in the city and housed equipment to convert high-voltage electricity to the 600-volt current used by the Los Angeles Railway's Yellow Cars.
Declared:12/20/1988 *(pg. 197)*

HCM #405
(Site of) PACIFIC ELECTRIC PICOVER RAILWAY STATION
16710 Sherman Way, Reseda (originally located in Marian, now Reseda; relocated to Picover Trolley stop between Hayvenhurst Avenue and Balboa Boulevard in 1917). Originally a small passenger station, the building was moved and renovated with additions several times over the years. It was moved to its present location in 1932 and served passengers until the line was abandoned in 1938. It was destroyed by fire in 1990.
Declared: 1/11/1989 *(pg. 257)*

HCM #406
MAGIC CASTLE
7001 Franklin Avenue, Hollywood. When they built the castle in 1909 as the residence of Rollin B. Lane, architects Dennis & Farwell adapted the design from a residence in Redlands known as Kimberly Crest. The style combines French Chateau and Gothic imagery.
Declared: 1/17/1989 *(pg. 136)*

HCM #407
SEYLER RESIDENCE
2305 Scarff Street, Los Angeles. Built in 1894, this Queen Anne house designed by Abraham M. Edelman is typical of the period.
Declared: 1/20/1989 *(pg. 329)*

HCM #408
SEAMAN HOUSE
2341 Scarff Street, Los Angeles. Built in 1888, the residence is a classic Queen Anne.
Declared: 1/20/1989 *(pg. 318)*

HCM #409
BURKHALTER RESIDENCE
2309-2311 Scarff Street, Los Angeles. Built in 1895, this Queen Anne house was the residence of Dennis Burkhalter, division superintendent of the Southern Pacific Railroad.
Declared: 1/20/1989 *(pg. 323)*

HCM #410
DISTRIBUTION STATION No. 31
1035 West 24th Street, Los Angeles. Built in 1925, this is a classic example of an industrial building of the period. It was designed by staff architects of the Pacific Gas & Electric Company.
Declared: 1/20/1989 *(pg. 317)*

HCM #411
ROBERT EDMUND WILLIAMS HOUSE (HATHAWAY HOME FOR CHILDREN)
840 North Avenue 66, Garvanza. This Craftsman house by local architect Robert Edmund Williams features stained glass designed by the Judson Studios.
Declared: 1/18/1989 *(pg. 197)*

HCM #412
GARVANZA PUMPING STATION AND (site of) HIGHLAND RESERVOIR
420 North Avenue 62, Garvanza. The Highland Reservoir was constructed before 1886 and is the oldest water storage site still serving Los Angeles. It had a capacity of 20.5 million gallons spread over four-and-one-half acres and was covered with a multi-gabled roof to prevent evaporation. The reservoir has been replaced with a tank, the roof design simulating the original.
Declared: 1/20/1989 *(pg. 172)*

HCM #413
OCTAGON HOUSE
Heritage Square, 3800 Homer Street, Los Angeles (original location on San Pasqual Avenue, Pasadena; relocated to 1917 Allen Street, Pasadena in 1917). Built in 1893 by Gilbert Longfellow and moved to Heritage Square in 1986, it is one of two eight-sided houses remaining in California and the only one in Southern California. Octagonal house design was briefly in vogue in the 19th century. Open to the public. Declared: 1/20/1989 *(pg. 171)*

HCM #414
WILMINGTON CEMETERY
605 East "O" Street, Wilmington. A gift of Phineas Banning in 1857, gravesites include those of Civil War soldiers and members of the Banning and Narbonne families. Declared: 1/24/1989 *(pg. 272)*

HCM #415
WILSHIRE BRANCH LIBRARY
149 North St. Andrews Place, Los Angeles. Built in 1926, the library was designed by Allan K. Ruoff using motifs from medieval structures. Declared: 2/1/1989 *(pg. 401)*

HCM #416
ZIEGLER ESTATE
4601 North Figueroa Street, Highland Park. Built in 1904 and designed by Alfred P. Wilson and Charles Hornbeck, this large residence, with its arroyo stone wall, mixes late Queen Anne ideas with Craftsman and Shingle styles. Declared: 2/21/1989 *(pg. 183)*

HCM #417
GORDON L. McDONOUGH HOUSE
2532 5th Avenue, Los Angeles. Designed in 1908 by local architect Frank M. Tyler, this Craftsman residence's interiors display the paneling, carpentry and brickwork typical of the Arts and Crafts movement. Declared: 2/21/1989 *(pg. 332)*

HCM #418
(Site of) GEORGE W. WILSON ESTATE
616 North Avenue 66, Garvanza. The residence was designed by the local firm of Eisen & Hunt in the Classical Revival style. An addition of a semi-circular porch nine years later by architects Train & Williams gave the house a more formal appearance. This structure was destroyed by fire in December 1989. Declared: 2/17/1989 *(pg. 197)*

HCM #419
WALKER MANSION
3300 West Adams Boulevard, Los Angeles. Architect Charles Whittlesey designed this Craftsman mansion on a grand scale with Tudor, Mediterranean and Mission Revival influences for William Barker, president of Barker Brothers, in 1908. Declared: 3/3/1989 *(pg. 319)*

HCM #420
MILBANK/McFIE ESTATE
3340 Country Club Drive / 1130 Arlington Avenue, Los Angeles. Built and designed in 1913 by the G. Laurence Stimson Company of Pasadena, the estate consists of two residences, their outbuildings and surrounding landscaped grounds. The two-story (plus basement and attic) mansion, of frame-and-hollow-tile veneer construction with Italianate details, was the residence of capitalist Isaac Milbank, president of Country Club Park. The interior features notable public rooms and a monumental stair hall. The second residence is in the American Colonial Revival style. Declared:12/13/1989 *(pg. 304)*

HCM #421
LAKE HOLLYWOOD RESERVOIR AND MULHOLLAND DAM
2460 Lake Hollywood Drive, Hollywood Hills. The concrete arch dam was designed by William Mulholland and constructed in 1923. Primarily a functional structure, Mulholland also intended it to be an aesthetic municipal monument in Mission style using graceful arches, buttresses and the California bear head across the façade. Declared: 3/31/1989 *(pg. 135)*

HCM #422
SILVER LAKE AND IVANHOE RESERVOIRS
Between West Silver Lake Drive and Silver Lake Boulevard, Silver Lake. Still in use, the Silver Lake reservoir was built in 1906. The capacity of the two reservoirs is 767 million gallons, which in 1906 could supply the city for twenty days. Declared: 3/31/1989 *(pg. 288)*

HCM #423
APARTMENT BUILDING
607 South Burnside Avenue, Los Angeles. Built in 1931, the residential building is designed in the Chateau style with Gothic influences. Declared: 3/31/1989 *(pg. 230)*

HCM #424
APARTMENT BUILDING
626 South Burnside Avenue, Los Angeles. Built in 1930, this apartment building features an Art Deco façade by architect Max Maltman. Declared: 3/31/1989 *(pg. 215)*

HCM #425
APARTMENT BUILDING
636 South Burnside Avenue, Los Angeles. Built in 1930 and designed by architect Max Maltman, this building is an apartment house with a stucco Art Deco façade. Declared: 3/31/1989 *(pg. 228)*

HCM #426
APARTMENT BUILDING
654 South Burnside Avenue, Los Angeles. Built in 1933, this Spanish Colonial Revival multi-level apartment building was designed by Milton J. Black. A significant feature of this structure, which ranges from two to four stories, is the cascade of tiled roofs. Declared: 3/31/1989 *(pg. 218)*

HCM #427
APARTMENT BUILDING
364 South Cloverdale Avenue, Los Angeles. Built in 1930 and designed by architect Clarence J. Smale, this apartment building features an Art Deco façade. Declared: 4/7/1989 *(pg. 222)*

HCM #428
VILLA CINTRA
430 South Cloverdale Avenue, Los Angeles. This building is a Spanish Colonial Revival apartment court constructed in 1928. Declared: 4/7/1989 *(pg. 222)*

HCM #429
APARTMENT BUILDING
601 South Cloverdale Avenue, Los Angeles. Built in 1928, this French-influenced building was designed by Leland Bryant. Declared: 4/7/1989 *(pg. 217)*

HCM #430
CORNELL APARTMENTS
603 South Cochran Avenue, Los Angeles. Built in 1928 and designed by architect Max Maltman, this four-story building includes Tudor elements. Declared: 4/7/1989 *(pg. 226)*

HCM #431
RESIDENCE
1851 West 11th Street, Los Angeles (original location on the 1000 block of South Olive Street). Built in approximately 1890, this residence is a classic example of the Queen Anne architecture popular in Los Angeles in the late 1800s. Designed by Robert Brown Young, it was moved to its present location in 1909. Declared: 5/5/1989 *(pg. 414)*

HCM #432
DORIA APARTMENTS
1600 West Pico Boulevard, Los Angeles. Built circa 1905 and designed by Gotfred Hanson for Doria Deighton Jones, this Mission Revival building featured retail space on the ground floor and apartments above. Declared: 5/5/1989 *(pg. 395)*

HCM #433
ALPHONSE J. FORGET RESIDENCE
1047 South Bonnie Brae Street, Los Angeles. Designed by architect Robert Brown Young, this home is a classic example of Queen Anne residential architecture. Declared: 5/5/1989 *(pg. 416)*

HCM #434
COLONEL JOHN E. STEARNS RESIDENCE
27 St. James Park, Los Angeles. Built in 1900 and designed by architect John Parkinson, this is a Classical Revival residence. Declared: 5/16/1989 *(pg. 339)*

HCM #435
ANDALUSIA APARTMENTS AND GARDENS
1471-1475 Havenhurst Drive, Los Angeles. Built in 1927, these Spanish Revival apartments were designed by Arthur and Nina Zwebell. Declared: 5/16/1989 *(pg. 354)*

HCM #436
HOWARD/NAGIN RESIDENCE
146 South Fuller Avenue, Los Angeles. Built in 1929 and designed by Paul R. Williams, this building is an English-influenced brick, stucco and wood, single-family residence. Declared: 5/19/1989 *(pg. 217)*

HCM #437
(Site of) A.H. JUDSON ESTATE
4911 Sycamore Terrace, Highland Park. Built in 1895, it was designed by George H. Wyman, known for the Bradbury Building (HCM #6), and built for Albert H. Judson who, with his partner George W. Morgan, subdivided Highland Park in 1885 (demolished 1992). Declared: 5/19/1989 *(pg. 189)*

HCM #438
APARTMENT BUILDING
445 South Detroit Street, Los Angeles. Constructed in 1932, this structure shows the influence of Mediterranean design.
Declared: 5/19/1989 *(pg. 225)*

HCM #439
APARTMENT BUILDING
450 South Detroit Street, Los Angeles. This Norman Revival courtyard building was constructed in 1926.
Declared: 5/19/1989 *(pg. 220)*

HCM #440
EASTERN STAR HOME, FRONT GROUNDS AND COURTYARD
11725 West Sunset Boulevard, Los Angeles. Built in 1931 and designed by William Mooser of San Francisco, the structure is Spanish Colonial Revival.
Declared: 5/16/1989 *(pg. 372)*

HCM #441
DUNNING HOUSE
5552 Carlton Way, Hollywood. Built in 1905 in the tradition of the American farmhouse, this wood-frame house has a clapboard exterior and a gabled roof.
Declared: 5/31/1989 *(pg. 137)*

HCM #442
ALBION COTTAGES AND MILAGRO MARKET
1801-1813 Albion Street, Lincoln Heights. Built in 1875, this complex (in addition to the neighborhood market) served as housing for construction workers on the Southern Pacific Railroad.
Declared: 6/20/1989 *(pg. 108)*

HCM #443
BOWMAN RESIDENCE
2425 Griffin Avenue, Lincoln Heights. This Eastlake home was built circa 1885.
Declared: 6/20/1989 *(pg. 111)*

HCM #444
OCTAVIUS W. MORGAN RESIDENCE
181 South Alta Vista Boulevard, Los Angeles. Built in 1929, this Spanish Colonial Revival belonged to a principal in the Los Angeles architectural firm of Morgan, Walls & Clements.
Declared: 6/20/1989 *(pg. 229)*

HCM #445
COURTNEY DESMOND ESTATE
1803-1811 Courtney Avenue, Los Angeles. Built in 1927, this Mediterranean villa was designed by Frank Harding and George Adams.
Declared: 6/20/1989 *(pg. 139)*

HCM #446
COURTYARD APARTMENT COMPLEX
10830 Lindbrook Drive, Westwood. Built in 1936 from a design by Frederic Clark, this Spanish Colonial Revival multi-family structure acts as a transition between the Westwood Village commercial areas and the single-family neighborhoods to the east.
Declared: 8/1/1989 *(pg. 369)*

HCM #447
COURTYARD APARTMENT COMPLEX
10836-10840 Lindbrook Drive, Westwood. These 1935 units designed by A.W. Angel are in the Monterey style.
Declared: 8/1/1989 *(pg. 357)*

HCM #448
WHITLEY COURT
1720-1728 Whitley Avenue, Hollywood. Built in 1919 and designed by Dennis & Farwell, this court consists of a grouping of four Dutch Colonial Revival buildings around a central garden with a Craftsman house, circa 1903, in the rear. This court's Bungalow style was once ubiquitous in the Hollywood area.
Declared:12/13/1988 *(pg. 138)*

HCM #449
PALACE THEATER
630 South Broadway, Los Angeles. Built in 1911, the six-story late Italian Renaissance structure, with a Classical French auditorium, was built by the Orpheum Theater & Realty Company and is the oldest surviving theater from this famous circuit. It was designed by architects G. Albert Lansburgh and Robert Brown Young with façade panels by sculptor Domingo Mora. The façade is notable as the first in Los Angeles to incorporate polychrome terra cotta as a decorative medium.
Declared: 8/16/1989 *(pg. 56)*

HCM #450
TOWER THEATER
800 South Broadway / 218, 224, 230 West 8th Street, Los Angeles. This 1927 terra cotta-clad building was designed by theater architect S. Charles Lee. It is his first theater design using French elements, and the first theater built in downtown Los Angeles with provision for sound films.
Declared: 8/16/1989 *(pg. 56)*

HCM #451
THE DARKROOM
(façade only)
5370 Wilshire Boulevard, Los Angeles. This façade is a rare example of Programmatic architecture. It was designed in 1938 by Marcus Miller to resemble a nine-foot-high Argus 35mm camera.
Declared:10/17/1989 *(pg. 223)*

HCM #452
FELIPE DE NEVE
BRANCH LIBRARY
2820 West 6th Street, Los Angeles. The library is a 1929 brick building in which architect Austin Whittlesey combines elements of Mediterranean and Spanish Colonial Revival styles.
Declared:10/17/1989 *(pg. 391)*

HCM #453
ARTISAN'S PATIO COMPLEX
6727-6733 Hollywood Boulevard, Hollywood. Built in 1914 and designed by Morgan, Walls & Clements, this is the only historic courtyard on Hollywood Boulevard.
Declared:10/17/1989 *(pg. 140)*

HCM #454
CHOUINARD INSTITUTE OF
THE ARTS
743 South Grandview Street, Los Angeles. Built in 1929 from designs by the firm of Morgan, Walls & Clements, this Art Deco structure housed the Chouinard Art Institute. This neighborhood was notable for the concentration of three major art schools, including Otis Art Institute and the Art Center School of Design.
Declared:10/24/1989 *(pg. 398)*

HCM #455
MARGARET T. AND BETTIE
MEAD CREIGHTON
RESIDENCE
2342 Scarff Street, Los Angeles. This early Colonial Revival residence was built in 1896.
Declared:10/24/1989 *(pg. 346)*

HCM #456
EZRA T. STIMSON HOUSE
839 West Adams Boulevard, Los Angeles. In 1901, this large Tudor Revival house was designed by architect Frederick Roehrig and built for Ezra T. Stimson.
Declared:10/24/1989 *(pg. 337)*

HCM #457
FREEMAN G. TEED HOUSE
2365 Scarff Street, Los Angeles. In 1893 this Craftsman home was built for Freeman G. Teed, who held various offices in the Los Angeles city government.
Declared:10/24/1989 *(pg. 303)*

HCM #458
WELLS-HALLIDAY MANSION
2146 West Adams Boulevard, Los Angeles. Built in 1901 in a Dutch Colonial style, this mansion was expanded in 1909 with a Craftsman wing.
Declared:11/3/1989 *(pg. 348)*

HCM #459
HAMBURGER'S
DEPARTMENT STORE (MAY
COMPANY–DOWNTOWN)
801-829 South Broadway, Los Angeles. Built in 1907 and designed by Alfred F. Rosenheim, this is a six-story, steel-frame Beaux Arts building.
Declared:10/17/1989 *(pg. 57)*

HCM #460
MAYAN THEATER
1044 South Hill Street, Los Angeles. Designed in 1927 by Morgan, Walls & Clements with Mayan decorations by Francisco Cornejo, this theater was intended to house live musical comedy presentations.
Declared:10/17/1989 *(pg. 53)*

HCM #461
(Site of) MEYERS HOUSE
4340 Eagle Rock Boulevard, Eagle Rock (original location at 5902 Pasadena Avenue, Highland Park). Built in the 1880s, this Colonial Revival residence was moved to its present location in the early 1920s. It was destroyed by fire in 1992.
Declared:11/3/1989 *(pg. 211)*

HCM #462
HOLLYWOOD AMERICAN
LEGION POST 43
2035 North Highland Avenue, Hollywood. Designed in 1929 by the firm of Weston & Weston, the building with its Egyptian Revival design and its location combine to create a prominent landmark.
Declared:11/3/1989 *(pg. 141)*

HCM #463
AFTON ARMS APARTMENTS
6141 Afton Place, Los Angeles. Designed in 1924 by the local architect Leland A. Bryant, it is Mission Revival in style.
Declared:11/3/1989 *(pg. 157)*

HCM #464
FARGO HOUSE
206 Thorne Street, Garvanza. In 1908, this wood-frame Craftsman house was built by a co-founder of the Wells Fargo business. It was designed by Harry Grey.
Declared:11/3/1989 *(pg. 167)*

HCM #465
SYCAMORE TREES
Located on Bienveneda Avenue (south from Sunset Boulevard to the cul-de-sac), Pacific Palisades. These 51 trees were planted during 1926 as part of the improvements of the subdivision.
Declared:10/27/1989 *(pg. 367)*

HCM #466
HENRY J. FOSTER RESIDENCE
1030 West 23rd Street, Los Angeles. This Queen Anne residence was built circa 1889.
Declared:10/27/1989 *(pg. 321)*

HCM #467
CHALET APARTMENTS
2375 Scarff Street, Los Angeles. Built in 1913 and designed by architect Frank M. Tyler, this nineteen unit apartment complex was designed to look like a large single-family residence.
Declared:10/27/1989 *(pg. 323)*

HCM #468
SACRED HEART CHURCH
2210-2212 Sichel Street / 2801 Baldwin Street, Los Angeles. Built in 1893 and designed by Frank Capitan, Sacred Heart is one of the few remaining late-nineteenth century churches in Los Angeles. It has a significant Victorian Gothic Revival exterior with a transitional square tower (now without the upper stories and spire). It also features a historic stained glass window and an ornate altar.
Declared:12/5/1989 *(pg. 114)*

HCM #469
IVAR I. PHILLIPS DWELLING
4200 North Figueroa Street, Highland Park. In 1907 this Craftsman house was constructed by Ivar Phillips as a model home. Its design details include extensive use of arroyo stone, flared eaves, scroll-cut rafter ends, shingles and beveled siding.
Declared:12/20/1989 *(pg. 200)*

HCM #470
IVAR I. PHILLIPS RESIDENCE
4204 North Figueroa Street, Highland Park. In 1907 Ivar Phillips built this Craftsman-Influenced house using arroyo stone for the chimney and foundation. Phillips was both an architect and an attorney.
Declared:12/20/1989 *(pg. 185)*

HCM #471
ARGUS COURT
1760 Colorado Boulevard, Eagle Rock. Built in 1923 by the firm of Taylor & Taylor, these Tudor Revival apartments feature open eaves and decorative half-timbering on the exterior.
Declared:12/20/1989 *(pg. 212)*

HCM #472
RIALTO THEATER BUILDING MARQUEE, BOX OFFICE AND MARBLE ENTRY FLOOR
812 South Broadway, Los Angeles. This rare example of a 1930s rectangular marquee was constructed on the base of the 1923 original and includes a substantial amount of its neon elements. The Art Deco box office was designed by William Lee Woolett.
Declared:12/20/1989 *(pg. 59)*

HCM #473
APARTMENT BUILDING
613 South Ridgeley Drive, Los Angeles. Constructed in 1932, this Chateauesque stucco apartment building is two and three stories in height with a hip roof. Decorative triangular parapets, gabled dormers, turrets, finials and crenels add variety to the roof.
Declared:12/8/1989 *(pg. 225)*

HCM #474
THE LITTLE NUGGET
Travel Town, Griffith Park. This 85-foot-long Union Pacific Railroad streamlined passenger car was built in 1937 by the Pullman-Standard Car Manufacturing Co. Its interior is divided into two sections, one a club-lounge and the other a train crew dormitory. The lounge room was designed in Victorian style by artist Walt Kuhn.
Declared: 1/26/1990 *(pg. 283)*

HCM #475
HIGHLAND TOWERS APARTMENTS (formerly Highbourne Gardens Apartments)
1920-1928 North Highland Avenue, Hollywood. The five-story, L-shaped building was designed by the firms Selkirk & Stanbery and Morgan, Walls & Clements. Its primary façade, in a Mediterranean style, is organized into four horizontal zones: a subtly rusticated base, a plain three-story shaft, a slightly more detailed attic and a recessed penthouse.
Declared:10/16/1990 *(pg. 140)*

HCM #476
BELASCO THEATER
1046-1054 South Hill Street, Los Angeles. Completed in 1926, this six-story reinforced concrete structure was designed by the firm of Morgan, Walls & Clements. Its eclectic cast-stone decorations display Churrigueresque, Spanish Renaissance, Moorish and Gothic details. The shallow auditorium, specifically designed for legitimate drama, places all patrons within hearing distance of the stage.
Declared: 1/30/1990 *(pg. 58)*

HCM #477
BRIGGS RESIDENCE
3734 West Adams Boulevard, Los Angeles. Built in 1912 as an Alpine Craftsman home from plans by the firm of Hudson & Munsell, the house, designed to complement the adjacent residence, features a steep cross-gabled roof and massive interior brick chimney.
Declared: 1/30/1990 *(pg. 346)*

HCM #478
**GUASTI VILLA /
BUSBY BERKELEY ESTATE**
3500 West Adams Boulevard, Los Angeles. The imposing Beaux Arts and Italian Renaissance Revival structure is an excellent example of the mansions that once lined this street. Its original owner, Secundo Guasti, was a poor Italian immigrant who became the owner of the world's largest vineyard of the period. In 1910 he hired architects Hudson & Munsell to build this house which he sold to Hollywood director Busby Berkeley in 1936.
Declared: 1/30/1990 *(pg. 333)*

HCM #479
**DR. GRANDVILLE
MacGOWAN HOME**
3726 West Adams Boulevard, Los Angeles. The mansion was built in 1912 from a design by the firm of Hudson & Munsell. It is an excellent example of Alpine Craftsman with Tudor Revival influences. Dr. MacGowan was the first commissioner of the Los Angeles Health Department.
Declared: 1/30/1990 *(pg. 311)*

HCM #480
SPANISH-AMERICAN WAR MEMORIAL
Pershing Square, Los Angeles. Completed in 1900, the life-size granite statue depicts a soldier standing at parade rest and personifies the eternal peace of the 21 young men from Southern California who died while serving in the 7th Regiment during the Spanish-American War. Sculpted in a representational style by S.M. Goddard, each soldier's uniform is realistically detailed.
Declared: 3/23/1990 *(pg. 57)*

HCM #481
MAUER HOUSE
932 Rome Drive, Mt. Washington. Designed in 1947 by architect John Lautner in the International Style, it was Lautner's third residential commission and features an irregular floor plan, large expanses of glass and an industrial roof-framing system that allowed rafters to be installed before walls.
Declared: 3/23/1990 *(pg. 194)*

HCM #482
ARTHUR S. BENT HOUSE
161 South Avenue 49, Highland Park. Built in 1904, this home, designed by architects Sumner P. Hunt and A. Wesley Eager in the Prairie style with Tudor half-timber detailing, is one of the earliest examples of Modernism in Southern California.
Declared: 5/1/1987 *(pg. 180)*

HCM #483
J.B. MERRILL HOUSE
815 Elyria Drive, Mt. Washington. Built in 1909 from a design by architect H.M. Patterson, it was one of the first homes on Mt. Washington. It is an example of a Shingle style Craftsman bungalow.
Declared: 3/23/1990 *(pg. 211)*

HCM #484
OAKRIDGE
18650 Devonshire Street, Northridge. Built in 1937, Oakridge was designed by architect Paul R. Williams in the English Manor style for actress Barbara Stanwyck. Theater and movie entertainer Jack Oakie purchased the home from Stanwyck a short time later.
Declared: 3/23/1990 *(pg. 249)*

HCM #485
NICOLOSI ESTATE
414 Saint Pierre Road, Los Angeles. Built in 1931 and designed by Paul R. Williams in the Mediterranean Revival style, the mansion's spectacular grounds include a serpentine swimming pool three hundred feet in length.
Declared: 4/6/1990 *(pg. 364)*

HCM #486
19th CENTURY LOS ANGELES CHINESE CEMETERY SHRINE
Evergreen Cemetery, 204 North Evergreen Avenue, Boyle Heights. Constructed in 1888, it consists of twin ceremonial burners flanking a central altar. It is one of the oldest Chinese-built structures in Los Angeles. Declared: 8/31/1990 *(pg. 112)*

HCM #487
SANCHEZ RANCH
3725 Don Felipe Drive, Los Angeles. Portions of the adobe structures were built in the 1790s as part of the *Rancho La Cienega o Paso de la Tijera.* Archaeological evidence indicates a prehistoric Native American village on this site. Declared: 5/1/1990 *(pg. 21)*

HCM #488
CANOGA PARK SOUTHERN PACIFIC RAILROAD STATION (formerly Owensmouth)
21355 Sherman Way, Canoga Park. Built in 1912, it is one of the few surviving Spanish Revival railroad stations. The structure was extensively damaged by fire in 1995. Declared: 5/30/1990 *(pg. 232)*

HCM #489
RICHARD H. ALEXANDER RESIDENCE
2119 Estrella Avenue, Los Angeles. Richard H. Alexander was a lieutenant colonel in the Army. His house, built circa 1888, was designed in Eastlake-style. Declared: 5/30/1990 *(pg. 314)*

HCM #490
SA-ANGNA
4231-4363 South Lincoln Boulevard and Admiralty Way, Los Angeles (a portion of the Oxford Triangle Property). The site was a major village and burial ground circa 1540 of the Gabrieleño Indians and contains remains of tools, jewelry and weapons. Declared: 5/1/1990 *(pg. 375)*

HCM #491
CHARLES B. BOOTH RESIDENCE AND CARRIAGE HOUSE
824 South Bonnie Brae Street, Los Angeles. Built in 1893 and designed by James H. Bradbeer, the buildings are an unusual combination of Colonial Revival and Moorish architecture. Declared: 7/13/1990 *(pg. 400)*

HCM #492
ARROYO SECO BANK BUILDING
6301 North Figueroa Street, Highland Park. Built in 1926 by the firm of Austin & Ashley, this building is an example of Renaissance Revival architecture. Declared: 7/13/1990 *(pg. 168)*

HCM #493
CASA DE ADOBE
4605 North Figueroa Street, Highland Park. Designed by Theodore Eisen as a museum for the Hispanic Society, this 1917 adobe was completely hand-built by Jose Velazquez and features a central courtyard and fountain. Declared: 7/13/1990 *(pg. 209)*

HCM #494
KELMAN RESIDENCE AND CARRIAGE BARN
5029 Echo Street, Highland Park. Built in 1911 and designed by Carl Gould and Charles Barkelew, it is an archetype of the California Craftsman bungalow with exterior shingle siding and fine interior woodwork. Declared: 7/13/1990 *(pg. 205)*

HCM #495
EL CAPITAN THEATRE
6834 Hollywood Boulevard, Hollywood. Built in 1926, the auditorium was designed by architect G. Albert Lansburgh in an East Indian Revival style. The exterior is Spanish Baroque Revival and was designed by the firm of Morgan, Walls & Clements. Declared: 6/12/1990 *(pg. 138)*

HCM #496
LYCURGUS LINDSAY MANSION (POLISH PARISH)
3424 West Adams Boulevard, Los Angeles. Built circa 1900 and designed by architect Charles F. Whittlesey, this massive house is Mission Revival in style. The distinctive exterior tiles used came from Western Art Tile Works, which was owned by Lindsay. Declared: 5/30/1990 *(pg. 333)*

HCM #497
CHARLES CLIFFORD GIBBONS RESIDENCE
2124 Bonsallo Avenue, Los Angeles. Built in 1892 and designed by architect J.H. Bradbeer, the home is a notable Queen Anne. Declared: 6/12/1990 *(pg. 338)*

HCM #498
LOIS ELLEN ARNOLD RESIDENCE
1978 Estrella Avenue, Los Angeles. This Queen Anne residence was built in 1888. Declared: 6/12/1990 *(pg. 299)*

HCM #499
AGNES B. HEIMGARTNER RESIDENCE
1982 Bonsallo Avenue, Los Angeles. Constructed in 1893, the residence is in the Eastlake style. Declared: 6/12/1990 *(pg. 318)*

HCM #500
JOHN B. KANE RESIDENCE
2122 Bonsallo Avenue, Los Angeles. Built in 1892 as an Eastlake cottage, it was designed by architect Fred R. Dorn. Declared: 6/12/1990 *(pg. 326)*

HCM #501
MICHAEL SHANNON RESIDENCE
1970 Bonsallo Avenue, Los Angeles. Built circa 1890, this is an Eastlake-style townhouse. Declared: 6/12/1990 *(pg. 309)*

HCM #502
FURTHMANN MANSION
3801 Lenawee Avenue, Los Angeles. The mansion is an excellent example of circa 1920 Neo-classicism. Screenwriter Jules Furthmann (*Mutiny on the Bounty* and *The Big Sleep*) lived here for many years in the early 1930s. Declared: 6/20/1990 *(pg. 19)*

HCM #503
WACHTEL STUDIO-HOME AND EUCALYPTUS GROVE
315 West Avenue 43, Mt. Washington. This Craftsman bungalow was constructed in 1906 from a design by its owner, Elmer Wachtel. He and his wife, Marion Kavanagh Wachtel, were prominent landscape painters associated with the Arroyo Arts Movement that flourished in the early 20th century. Declared:10/9/1990 *(pg. 186)*

HCM #504
BARLOW SANATORIUM (buildings and grounds)
2000 Stadium Way, Los Angeles. Founded in 1902 by Dr. Walter Jarvis Barlow as a tuberculosis sanatorium, it was the first such institution in the city. Between 1902 and 1927 several Los Angeles-area families, including the Lankershims, the Van Nuys and the Newhalls, donated funds for buildings. The complex consists of many noteworthy structures including Birge Hall, designed by architect B.B. Bixby. Declared:10/9/1990 *(pg. 101)*

HCM #505
FIRST BAPTIST CHURCH OF SAN PEDRO
555 West 7th Street, San Pedro. Built in 1919 and designed by architect Norman Marsh in the Beaux Arts style, this building features Egyptian columns and fine stained glass windows. Declared: 5/22/1990 *(pg. 269)*

HCM #506
TISCHLER RESIDENCE
175 Greenfield Avenue, Los Angeles. Built in 1950 by architect Rudolph Schindler in the International Style, this house is noted forthe unusual geometrical arrangement of its street-façade walls and windows. Declared:10/9/1990 *(pg. 362)*

HCM #507
HIRAM V. SHORT RESIDENCE
2110 Estrella Avenue, Los Angeles. Built in 1888, the home is an excellent example of Eastlake architecture with Italianate influence. Declared:11/2/1990 *(pg. 331)*

HCM #508
GILMORE GASOLINE SERVICE STATION
859 North Highland Avenue, Hollywood. Built for the Gilmore Oil Company in 1935, the Art Deco structure was designed by engineer R.J. Kadow. Declared: 3/23/1992 *(pg. 214)*

HCM #509
CAMPHOR TREES
1200 Block of Lakme Avenue, Wilmington. Originally part of the Phineas Banning Estate, these 52 trees are survivors of the group planted when the Banning heirs sold the land for subdivision in 1930. Declared:12/18/1990 *(pg. 269)*

HCM #510
RESIDENCE
1157 West 55th Street, Los Angeles. Built in 1913 from a design by Fred E. Edmison, this is a wood shingle Craftsman house with Oriental influence. Declared: 1/11/1991 *(pg. 58)*

HCM #511
RESIDENCE
1100 West 55th Street, Los Angeles. Built in 1911 and designed by E.A. Eastman, this Craftsman house is significant because of its grand scale and fine detailing. Declared: 1/11/1991 *(pg. 61)*

HCM #512
CHURCH OF THE ADVENT
4976 West Adams Boulevard, Los Angeles. Built in 1925 from a design by architect Arthur B. Benton in a Gothic Craftsman style, it was his last church commission. Declared: 1/16/1991 *(pg. 312)*

HCM #513
SOUTHERN CALIFORNIA EDISON SERVICE YARD STRUCTURE
615 East 108th Street, Los Angeles. This 1930 Mediterranean brick building has a Spanish-tiled hip roof. Declared: 1/15/1991 *(pg. 62)*

HCM #514
RESIDENCE
383 10th Street, San Pedro. Built in 1907, this Colonial Revival house uses three types of wood siding. Declared: 1/22/1991 *(pg. 271)*

HCM #515
BATTERY OSGOOD-FARLEY
Fort MacArthur Upper Reservation, 3601 Gaffey Street, San Pedro. Built in 1919, this massive concrete bunker was an important part of United States coastal artillery defense through 1944. Declared: 1/22/1991 *(pg. 273)*

HCM #516
ST. JOHN'S EPISCOPAL CHURCH
514 West Adams Boulevard, Los Angeles. Constructed in 1924 from a design by brothers F. Pierpont Davis and Walter Davis, the structure was modeled after two Italian churches. The bas-reliefs in tufa stone on the west façade are by S. Cartiano Scarpitta. Declared: 1/22/1991 *(pg. 336)*

HCM #517
RESIDENCE
917 East 49th Place, Los Angeles. Built in 1885, it is an Eastlake style house. Declared: 1/16/1991 *(pg. 59)*

HCM #518
RESIDENCE
1207 East 55th Street, Los Angeles. Designed by George Sills, the residence has an unusual masonry veneer. Declared: 1/16/1991 *(pg. 63)*

HCM #519
COCKINS HOUSE
2653 South Hoover Street, Los Angeles. Built in 1894, this Queen Anne house was designed by the firm of Bradbeer & Ferris. Declared: 2/1/1991 *(pg. 344)*

HCM #520
EL REY THEATRE
5515-5519 Wilshire Boulevard, Los Angeles. This Art Deco neighborhood movie theater was built in 1936 to designs by Clifford Balch. Declared: 2/26/1991 *(pg. 224)*

HCM #521
TAGGART HOUSE
5423 Black Oak Drive, Hollywood Hills. Built in 1922, it was designed by Lloyd Wright in an Expressionist Modern style. Declared: 3/15/1991 *(pg. 142)*

HCM #522
STATE THEATRE BUILDING
701-713 South Broadway / 300-314 West 7th Street, Los Angeles. Designed by the firm of Weeks & Day in 1921 for the Loews circuit, it has a steel-reinforced concrete structure decorated in the Plateresque style. Declared: 3/20/1991 *(pg. 61)*

HCM #523
UNITED ARTISTS THEATER BUILDING
927-939 South Broadway, Los Angeles. The theater, constructed by the United Artists Corporation, was the only major preview house built by the company in Los Angeles rather than in New York City. Designed by the firm of Walker & Eisen (building) and C.H. Crane (theater) and built in 1927 in a Spanish Gothic style, it stands as a tribute to film notables Mary Pickford, Douglas Fairbanks, Charlie Chaplin and D.W. Griffith who established United Artists in 1919. Declared: 3/20/1991 *(pg. 60)*

HCM #524
CAMEO THEATER (formerly Clune's Broadway)
526-530 South Broadway, Los Angeles. Designed by Alfred F. Rosenheim in a Beaux Arts interpretation of Italian Renaissance, the theater was constructed in 1910. When it closed in the early 1990s, it was the longest continually operational movie theater in the state. Its builder, William Clune, was one of the pioneers of the film production and distribution industry. Declared: 3/20/1991 *(pg. 62)*

HCM #525
ARCADE THEATER
532-536 South Broadway, Los Angeles. Built in 1910 from a design by Morgan & Walls, the Arcade features a classic Beaux Arts façade. The building marked the entry of vaudeville producer Alexander Pantages into Los Angeles and sparked the beginning of a thriving theater district.
Declared: 3/20//1991 *(pg. 65)*

HCM #526
ROXIE THEATER
512-524 South Broadway, Los Angeles. Built in 1931 from a design by John Cooper, the Roxie was one of the last film houses constructed in downtown Los Angeles and is the only Art Deco theater on Broadway.
Declared: 3/20/1991 *(pg. 54)*

HCM #527
RESIDENCE
1437 North Martel Avenue, Hollywood. This California Craftsman bungalow was built in 1914.
Declared: 4/2/1991 *(pg. 143)*

HCM #528
DR. FRANKLIN S. WHALEY RESIDENCE
6434 Crescent Street, Garvanza. Built in 1887, this house is one of the oldest homes in Garvanza. It is a textbook example of the Italianate style and still contains most of its original building fabric.
Declared: 4/23/1991 *(pg. 203)*

HCM #529
MONTECITO VIEW HOUSE
4115 Berenice Place, Montecito Heights. Built in 1909 and designed by Lester S. Moore, this Craftsman bungalow overlooks the Arroyo Seco.
Declared: 4/23/1991 *(pg. 174)*

HCM #530
JOHN ENTENZA HOUSE (CASE STUDY HOUSE #9)
205 Chautauqua Boulevard, Pacific Palisades. Built in 1949 and designed as a collaborative effort between Charles Eames and Eero Saarinen, this International Modern residence is the only example of Saarinen's work in Los Angeles. Entenza was the editor of *Arts and Architecture* magazine, which initiated the renowned Case Study House Program.
Declared: 4/30/1991 *(pg. 358)*

HCM #531
WILSHIRE WARD CHAPEL
1209 South Manhattan Place, Los Angeles. This 1928 Art Deco and Spanish edifice was designed by Harold Burton, the official architect of the Mormon Church.
Declared: 5/10/1991 *(pg. 349)*

HCM #532
VENICE ARCADES, COLUMNS AND CAPITALS
67-71 Windward Avenue, Venice. Constructed in 1904 by Abbot Kinney and designed by C.R. Russell, the arcades were patterned after those at the Piazza San Marco in Venice, Italy.
Declared: 4/23/1991 *(pg. 18)*

HCM #533
RESIDENCE
2660 Sichel Street, Lincoln Heights. The house was built in 1893 in the Eastlake style.
Declared: 6/11/1991 *(pg. 116)*

HCM #534
I. MAGNIN & CO. BUILDING
3240 Wilshire Boulevard, Los Angeles. Constructed in 1938, this Art Deco department store was designed by Myron Hunt and H.C. Chambers.
Declared: 6/11/1991 *(pg. 405)*

HCM #535
HOLLYWOODLAND'S GRANITE RETAINING WALLS AND INTERCONNECTING GRANITE STAIRS
Upper Beachwood Canyon, Hollywood Hills. Built circa 1923, the stairs are unique and important character-defining elements of this residential neighborhood.
Declared: 6/11/1991 *(pg. 128)*

HCM #536
EAGLE ROCK PLAYGROUND CLUBHOUSE
1100 Eagle Vista Drive, Eagle Rock. Built in 1953 by architect Richard Neutra and his son Dion, the building is in the International Style.
Declared: 7/2/1991 *(pg. 207)*

HCM #537
EAGLE ROCK WOMEN'S TWENTIETH CENTURY CLUBHOUSE
5101 Hermosa Avenue, Eagle Rock. Built in 1915 by the members' husbands, the clubhouse is one of the few large-scale Craftsman structures in Los Angeles.
Declared: 7/2/1991 *(pg. 208)*

HCM #538
DAVID J. WITMER FAMILY HOUSES AND COMPOUND
208, 210, 210 1/2 Witmer Street / 1422 West 2nd Street, Los Angeles. Dating from 1921 and constructed from an award-winning design by their owner and namesake, the houses are significant not only for their Mediterranean Revival design, but also for the poured-concrete method of construction, which was unusual for residences of the period. The Witmer family built the first cable car in Los Angeles and founded the California Bank. David Witmer was chief architect of the Pentagon in Washington.
Declared: 7/2/1991 *(pg. 411)*

HCM #539
J.E. MAXWELL RESIDENCE
211 South Avenue 52, Highland Park. Constructed in 1907, it was designed by Arthur B. Benton in the Craftsman style.
Declared: 7/19/1991 *(pg. 208)*

HCM #540
(Site of) PIPER HOUSE
326 North Avenue 53, Highland Park. This Craftsman home was constructed in 1905 by William Neely. It was destroyed by fire on August 20, 1995.
Declared: 7/19/1991 *(pg. 210)*

HCM #541
REV. WILLIEL THOMSON RESIDENCE
215 South Avenue 52, Highland Park. Built circa 1898, it is late Queen Anne in style.
Declared: 7/19/1991 *(pg. 170)*

HCM #542
SWANSON HOUSE
2373 Addison Way, Eagle Rock. Built in 1921 by Emil Swanson, the exterior half-pine siding resembles a log cabin. Mr. Swanson, founder of the Eagle Rock Lumber Co., endeavored to popularize this style of architecture, but to no avail.
Declared: 7/2/1991 *(pg. 183)*

HCM #543
FARMERS MARKET
Bordered by 3rd Street, Fairfax Avenue and Gilmore Lane, Los Angeles. Started in 1934 when the landlord provided hard-pressed Depression era farmers with a direct market outlet for their produce, the site also houses the 1852 Gilmore Adobe, one of the oldest homes in the city.
Declared: 7/24/1991 *(pg. 227)*

HCM #544
IRVINE / BYRNE BUILDING
249 South Broadway, Los Angeles. Built in 1895 and designed in the Beaux Arts style, this building is a five-story brick structure designed by Sumner Hunt.
Declared: 8/2/1991 *(pg. 64)*

HCM #545
HOLLYWOOD ROOSEVELT HOTEL
7000 Hollywood Boulevard, Hollywood. Built in 1926 from a design by architect H.B. Traver, this Spanish Colonial Revival structure is associated with the growth of the film industry and was built by investors Douglas Fairbanks, Marcut Lowe, Louis B. Mayer and Mary Pickford. The first Academy Awards ceremony was held here in 1929.
Declared: 8/13/1991 *(pg. 143)*

HCM #546
WESTLAKE THEATRE BUILDING
636 South Alvarado Street, Los Angeles. Designed by Richard D. Bates in the Spanish Colonial Revival style with Churrigueresque detailing, this is a two-story theater with a balcony, working stage and six retail stores.
Declared: 9/24/1991 *(pg. 406)*

HCM #547
CAMP JOSEPHO, MALIBU LODGE
3000 Rustic Canyon Road, Los Angeles. This redwood clapboard Craftsman lodge was built in 1941 for the Boy Scouts of America.
Declared:10/2/1991 *(pg. 361)*

HCM #548
KOREAN INDEPENDENCE MEMORIAL BUILDING
1368 West Jefferson Boulevard, Los Angeles. Completed in 1937, this structure served as United States headquarters for the Korean independence movement against the Japanese occupation. Since the end of the war, it has been a center for Korean cultural activities.
Declared:10/2/1991 *(pg. 304)*

HCM #549
HIGHLAND THEATRE BUILDING
5600 North Figueroa Street, Highland Park. A concrete structure in the Moorish taste designed by theater architect L.A. Smith, it is the only remaining theater on what was once Pasadena Avenue.
Declared:10/2/1991 *(pg. 201)*

HCM #550
A.J. MADISON HOUSE
148 South Avenue 56, Highland Park. Built in 1920 and designed by architect Arthur G. Lindley (best known for the Alex Theater in Glendale), this is a Prairie style residence.
Declared:10/2/1991 *(pg. 205)*

HCM #551
THOMAS W. PHILLIPS RESIDENCE
2215 South Harvard Boulevard, Los Angeles. Constructed in 1905 from a Craftsman design by the team of Hunt & Eager, the house is one of a small number of their remaining structures. The exterior colors, cast stone and trees date to 1905. Thomas W. Phillips was one of the founding residents of Los Angeles.
Declared:11/13/1991 *(pg. 341)*

HCM #552
EINAR C. PETERSEN
STUDIO COURT
4350-4352 3/4 Beverly
Boulevard, Los Angeles. It
was built in 1921 by its
namesake, an artist responsible for numerous murals in
downtown Los Angeles. The
Storybook style structure
resembles a street in the
town of Abeltoft, Denmark,
where Petersen was born.
The lot contains five stucco
buildings, some half-tim-
bered with gabled roofs
whose shingle patterns
evoke those of the thatched
roofs in Europe. This assem-
blage of buildings is significant because it is intact and
offers a rare architectural
style and quality of design
executed by an important
member of the 1920s Los
Angeles art community.
Declared:11/13/1991 *(pg. 410)*

HCM #553
MIDTOWN SCHOOL
4155 Russell Avenue, Los
Angeles. The only school
designed by architect John
Lautner, it was constructed
in 1960 in the International
Style. The four separate
pavilion classrooms feature a
low scale to suit children
and have laminated wood
roof beams and radiant floor
heating.
Declared:11/12/1991 *(pg. 289)*

HCM #554
LA PALOMA
369 North Avenue 53,
Highland Park. This Tudor
Craftsman residence was
designed by Edward
Symonds and constructed in
1907. Decorative half-timbering, leaded glass and a
spacious floor plan make this
one of Symonds's best
designs. The architect died
at the age of 27.
Declared: 3/18/1992 *(pg. 202)*

HCM #555
MOTHER TRUST SUPERET
CENTER
2512-2516 West 3rd Street,
Los Angeles. The headquarters of the church founded
by Josephine Trust, a faith
healer in the 1920s, was
designed by Carleton
Winslow. The center is significant for the chapel's
New England vernacular
architecture and because it
is a symbol of the growth of
non-traditional religion in
Los Angeles.
Declared: 3/18/1992 *(pg. 415)*

HCM #556
CHARLES AND NETTIE
WILLIAMS HOME
212-214 North Avenue 57,
Highland Park. The front
dwelling is an 1892 cottage.
The rear unit, built in 1905,
is a rare pre-Civil War style
board-and-batten house
designed by Henry W. Corns.
Declared: 4/21/1992 *(pg. 195)*

HCM #557
(Site of) WILBUR F. WOOD
HOUSE
4026 Bluff Place, San Pedro.
The house was owned by
the man known as the
"father of the modern tuna
packing industry," who
earned the sobriquet by
developing the method of
canning tuna still used
today. Through an amalga-
mation with other small
canneries, his company,
Chicken of the Sea, became
the largest tuna concern in
the nation.
Declared: 4/21/1992 *(pg. 273)*

HCM #558
DEPARTMENT OF WATER
AND POWER DISTRIBUTING
STATION No. 2
225 North Avenue 61,
Highland Park. Constructed
in 1916, the Greek Revival
structure displays symmetrical pedimented doors and a
projecting portico supported
by Tuscan columns. This was
the only Highland Park commission completed by architect Frederick L. Roehrig,
designer of the Green Hotel
in Pasadena.
Declared: 4/21/1992 *(pg. 202)*

HCM #559
13th CHURCH OF CHRIST,
SCIENTIST
1750 North Edgemont
Street, Los Angeles.
Designed by the firm of
Allison & Allison in the
Italian Renaissance Revival
style, this grand ecclesiastical
building was constructed
in 1926.
Declared: 4/21/1992 *(pg. 144)*

HCM #560
WRIGHT HOUSE
2121-2123 Bonsallo Avenue,
Los Angeles. Constructed in
1889, it features an exterior
clad with a combination of
shiplap siding and square
butt shingles.
Declared: 5/26/1992 *(pg. 301)*

HCM #561
ALLEN HOUSE
2125 Bonsallo Avenue, Los
Angeles. This 1889 home,
constructed with a clipped-
gable roof, one eyebrow
dormer and one conically-
roofed three-sided dormer, is
an example of the Shingle
style. Robert Allen, was a Los
Angeles city council member
in the 1920s.
Declared: 5/26/1992 *(pg. 332)*

HCM #562
EAGLE ROCK WOMEN'S CHRISTIAN TEMPERANCE UNION HOME FOR WOMEN
2235 Norwalk Avenue, Eagle Rock. A Mediterranean structure built in 1927 and designed by A. Godfrey Bailey, it includes a cruciform plan sited at a forty-five-degree angle to the street. The building has social significance as the sole physical reminder in Los Angeles of the Temperance and Women's Suffrage Movement.
Declared: 5/26/1992 *(pg. 203)*

HCM #563
HEADLEY/HANDLEY HOUSE
3003 Runyon Canyon Road, Hollywood Hills. Designed in 1945 by architect Lloyd Wright, the house was remodeled by Wright in 1966. The predominant form of the building is a two-story-high pyramidal shingle roof. Comparatively low fieldstone walls enclose bedroom wings below the high, central living space.
Declared: 7/14/1992 *(pg. 364)*

HCM #564
E.A. SPENCER ESTATE
5660 Ash Street, Highland Park. Built in 1898, the site contains a house, carriage barn, water tower and auto garage. The house is American Foursquare in style. Three of the structures were designed by architect Charles C. Dodge, and the stone garage was designed by architect Frederick M. Ashley.
Declared: 8/25/1992 *(pg. 204)*

HCM #565
CHARLES H. GREENSHAW RESIDENCE
1102 Lantana Drive, Garvanza. Built in 1906 and designed by architect Joseph Cather Newsom, the Mission Revival structure is surmounted by ornate gable ends on all four sides.
Declared: 8/25/1992 *(pg. 184)*

HCM #566
MAY COMPANY WILSHIRE (LOS ANGELES COUNTY MUSEUM OF ART)
6067 Wilshire Boulevard, Los Angeles. Constructed in 1939, the Streamline Moderne department store was designed by architect Albert C. Martin in association with Samuel A. Marx. Its most distinctive design element is a four-story gold mosaic quarter-cylinder at its southwest corner.
Declared: 9/30/1992 *(pg. 226)*

HCM #567
LITTLE COUNTRY CHURCH OF HOLLYWOOD
1750 North Argyle Avenue, Hollywood. Built in 1934 in the Classical Revival style from plans drawn by architect Paul Kingsbury, it is a physical record of a pre-World War II radio ministry church.
Declared:10/2/1992 *(pg. 133)*

HCM #568
THOMAS A. CHURCHILL, SR. RESIDENCE
215 South Wilton Place, Los Angeles. Built in 1909, this Craftsman home was designed by F. Pierpont Davis.
Declared:10/27/1992 *(pg. 402)*

HCM #569
VAN DE KAMP'S HOLLAND DUTCH BAKERY
3020 San Fernando Road, Los Angeles. Designed by architect J. Edwin Hopkins and constructed in 1930, this structure is the only example of a Dutch Renaissance Revival industrial plant in Los Angeles and was a very successful effort to establish a corporate image through thematic architecture.
Declared: 5/12/1992 *(pg. 187)*

HCM #570
AIRPORT THEME BUILDING
201 Center Way, Los Angeles. Constructed in 1961, this homage to the Space Age was built using two intersecting parabolic arches supporting a disc-shaped restaurant pod. The icon was designed by Charles Luckman, William Pereira, Welton Becket and Paul Williams.
Declared:12/18/1992 *(pg. 21)*

HCM #571
CABRILLO BEACH BATH HOUSE
3720 Stephen White Drive, San Pedro. Constructed in 1932 from a Mediterranean design by engineer David Berniker, it is the last beach bathhouse of the period in the city.
Declared:12/23/1992 *(pg. 268)*

HCM #572
WARNER BROTHERS HOLLYWOOD THEATRE
6433 Hollywood Boulevard, Hollywood. Completed in 1928 from a design by theater architect G. Albert Lansburgh, it is an Italianate and Beaux Arts retail, office and theater.
Declared: 2/9/1993 *(pg. 144)*

HCM #573
EL PORTAL THEATER
5265-5271 Lankershim Boulevard, North Hollywood. Completed in 1926, this Spanish Renaissance Revival retail, office and theater building was designed by theater architect L.A. Smith. Declared: 2/9/1993 *(pg. 233)*

HCM #574
PIERCE BROTHERS MORTUARY
714 West Washington Boulevard, Los Angeles. Begun in 1923, the Spanish Colonial Revival structure is by the architectural firm Meyer & Holler. Declared: 2/9/1993 *(pg. 295)*

HCM #575
SECURITY TRUST & SAVINGS BANK, HIGHLAND PARK BRANCH
5601 North Figueroa Street, Highland Park. Completed in 1923, this brick-and-concrete Renaissance Revival commercial structure was designed by architects John and Donald Parkinson. Declared: 2/9/1993 *(pg. 193)*

HCM #576
SHERATON TOWN HOUSE HOTEL AND NEON ROOF SIGN
2959-2973 Wilshire Boulevard, Los Angeles. A thirteen-story red brick and cast stone hotel, it was designed by Norman Alpaugh and built just before the stock market crash in 1929. The two neon roof signs read: "Sheraton Town House" and "Sheraton." Declared: 4/7/1993 *(pg. 407)*

HCM #577
STURGES HOUSE
441-449 Skyewiay Road, Los Angeles. This residence, planned in 1939 by Frank Lloyd Wright, is the only Usonian house in Southern California. Declared: 5/25/1993 *(pg. 377)*

HCM #578
EMANUEL DANISH EVANGELICAL LUTHERAN CHURCH
4254-4260 3rd Avenue, Los Angeles. Built in 1937, it was designed by Edith Northmann in the Dansk Landsby Kirke style. Northmann, born in Denmark, was perhaps the most prolific and respected female architect based in Los Angeles from the mid-1920s to 1940s. Declared: 5/25/1993 *(pg. 341)*

HCM #579
WATTLES PARK, MANSION AND GARDENS
1824-1850 North Curson Avenue, Hollywood. Built in 1907 and designed by Myron Hunt and Elmer Grey, the Wattles estate is typical of the winter homes built by wealthy Eastern families long before Hollywood became the movie capital of the world. It stands as one of the last remaining such estates in Hollywood. The mansion is in the Mission Revival style with an Italian Renaissance park and a Japanese garden. Declared: 5/25/1993 *(pg. 145)*

HCM #580
GOLDEN STATE MUTUAL LIFE INSURANCE BUILDING #1
4261 South Central Avenue, Los Angeles. Completed in 1929 and designed in the Spanish Renaissance Revival style by architect James H. Garrott, the building was home to one of the five largest African American-owned insurance companies in the United States. Declared: 6/29/1993 *(pg. 63)*

HCM #581
YORK BOULEVARD STATE BANK/BANK OF AMERICA AND STOREFRONTS
5057-5061 York Boulevard, Highland Park. Constructed in 1929 from a design by Carl J. Wey, this poured-concrete strcture is of Mediterranean style. Declared: 8/10/1993 *(pg. 180)*

HCM #582
W.F. POOR RESIDENCE
120 North Avenue 54, Highland Park. Built circa 1904, this Craftsman residence is attributed to Paul Van Trees. Declared: 8/10/1993 *(pg. 201)*

HCM #583
ZOBELEIN ESTATE
3738-3770 South Flower Street, Los Angeles. Built in 1937 and designed by architect W.L. Schmolle, it is Mediterranean in style. Declared: 9/21/1993 *(pg. 349)*

HCM #584
EGYPTIAN THEATRE
6706-6712 Hollywood Boulevard, Hollywood. Built in 1922, the theater was designed by Meyer & Holler. It was renovated in 1998 to house the American Cinematheque. Declared: 9/21/1993 *(pg. 146)*

HCM #585
OCCIDENTAL COLLEGE HALL OF LETTERS/ SAVOY APARTMENTS
121 North Avenue 50, Highland Park. Built in 1904, this unpainted masonry structure was designed in the Classical Revival style by the firm of Dennis & Farwell. It served for ten years as the main building for Occidental College, which moved to Eagle Rock in 1914. It is the only remaining structure from the Highland Park campus. Declared:10/15/1993 *(pg. 184)*

HCM #586
SAN FERNANDO PIONEER MEMORIAL CEMETERY
14400 Foothill Boulevard, Sylmar. A flat, 3.8 acre Sylmar site, the cemetery is covered with native grasses and includes a walkway and memorial patio. It is the second-oldest cemetery in the San Fernando Valley and holds the remains of early pioneers, Civil War veterans and Mission Indians.
Declared:11/30/1993 *(pg. 253)*

HCM #587
LINCOLN HEIGHTS JAIL/ LOS ANGELES CITY JAIL
(in two sections)
401-449 North Avenue 19, Lincoln Heights. The Art Deco portion of the jail was built in 1931 by the Los Angeles City Construction Department. The Bauhaus-inspired addition was built in 1949 from designs by Kaufman & Stanton.
Declared:11/30/1993 *(pg. 115)*

HCM #588
JANSS INVESTMENT COMPANY UPTOWN BRANCH OFFICE BUILDING (SOKOL HALL)
500-508 North Western Avenue, Los Angeles. Built in 1928, the building was designed by Percy Parke Lewis in a Byzantine style.
Declared:11/30/1993 *(pg. 145)*

HCM #589
FEUCHTWANGER HOUSE (VILLA AURORA)
520 Paseo Miramar, Pacific Palisades. Built in 1928, the Spanish Colonial Revival house was designed by Mark Daniels. Lion Feuchtwanger was a German Jew who escaped persecution during World War II. In addition to housing his enormous library, Feuchtwanger used his home as a refuge for talented émigrés.
Declared: 2/2/1994 *(pg. 378)*

HCM #590
BROOKLYN AVENUE NEIGHBORHOOD CORRIDOR
Cesar E. Chavez Avenue between Cummings Street and Mott Street, Boyle Heights. The corridor (formerly Brooklyn Avenue) symbolizes the western migration to Los Angeles from New York of a large number of Jewish immigrants who moved there in the early 20th century.
Declared: 3/8/1994 *(pg. 109)*

HCM #591
DENKER ESTATE
3820 West Adams Boulevard, Los Angeles. The Beaux Arts house was built in 1912 from a design by architect B. Cooper Corbett for Louise Denker, the widow of real estate tycoon Andrew Denker.
Declared: 3/8/1994 *(pg. 312)*

HCM #592
PHILOSOPHICAL RESEARCH SOCIETY, INC.
3910 Los Feliz Boulevard, Los Angeles. The building was constructed in the pre-Columbian style between 1936 and 1959 by Manly Palmer Hall, founder of the Society; the principal architect was Robert Stacy-Judd.
Declared: 3/8/1994 *(pg. 286)*

HCM #593
MAX FACTOR MAKE-UP SALON
1666 North Highland Avenue, Hollywood. This four-story concrete building was remodeled by theater architect S. Charles Lee into an Art Deco design with architectural elements typical of the English Regency period. Now a Hollywood history museum occupies the space.
Declared: 4/26/1994 *(pg. 147)*

HCM #594
BRADBURY HOUSE
102 Ocean Way, Pacific Palisades. Built circa 1922 from a design by John Byers, this adobe residence is a textbook example of Spanish Colonial Revival. The Bradbury family was one of the wealthiest families in the city at that time.
Declared: 4/26/1994 *(pg. 373)*

HCM #595
VENICE DIVISION POLICE STATION
685 Venice Boulevard, Venice. Built by the Bureau of Construction in the Art Deco style, it was completed in 1930.
Declared: 4/26/1994 *(pg. 16)*

HCM #596
PETROLEUM BUILDING
714 West Olympic Boulevard, Los Angeles. Designed by Meyer & Holler, it is reminiscent of early Renaissance Florentine palaces.
Declared: 4/26/1994 *(pg. 66)*

HCM #597
RAYMOND CHANDLER SQUARE
Intersection of Hollywood Boulevard and Cahuenga Boulevard, Hollywood. Located in the Hollywood Boulevard National Register Historic District, the square honors the Los Angeles author. Many of Chandler's works were written in his office on this square. The office of his detective Philip Marlowe was located in the fictional "Cahuenga Building, on Hollywood Boulevard, near Ivar."
Declared: 8/5/1994 *(pg. 146)*

HCM #598
BENJAMIN J. WATERS RESIDENCE
2289 West 25th Street, Los Angeles. Built in 1899 in the Colonial Revival style, it is one of the few remaining examples of Victorian architecture in the Arlington Heights area.
Declared: 9/27/1994 *(pg. 319)*

HCM #599
JULIUS BIERLICH RESIDENCE
1818 South Gramercy Place, Los Angeles. Designed in 1914 by architect Frank M. Tyler, it is is a California Craftsman bungalow.
Declared: 9/27/1994 *(pg. 350)*

HCM #600
LUCIEN AND BLANCHE GRAY RESIDENCE
2515 4th Avenue, Los Angeles. Built in 1909, this Craftsman home was designed by architect Arthur S. Heineman. The Community Chest (now the United Way) was founded in the living room of the Gray home.
Declared: 9/27/1994 *(pg. 316)*

HCM #601
GRAMERCY PARK HOMESTEAD
2102 West 24th Street, Los Angeles. Built in 1910, it was designed in a transitional Craftsman style by architect William E. Blaikie.
Declared: 9/27/1994 *(pg. 345)*

HCM #602
AUGUSTE MARQUIS RESIDENCE (FILIPINO FEDERATION OF AMERICA)
2302 West 25th Street, Los Angeles. Built in 1904, the residence combines Eastlake and Queen Anne influences.
Declared: 9/27/1994 *(pg. 342)*

HCM #603
VILLA VALLOMBROSA
2074 Watsonia Terrace, Los Angeles. Built in 1928, this home was designed by Nathan Coleman in the Tuscan Rural style.
Declared: 9/27/1994 *(pg. 149)*

HCM #604
HOLLYWOOD SCHOOL FOR GIRLS/WOMEN'S CLUB OF HOLLYWOOD
1741 North La Brea Avenue, Hollywood. Constructed in 1948 in the Spanish Colonial Revival style, the club was designed by Arthur E. Harvey.
Declared:11/1/1994 *(pg. 148)*

HCM #605
OLD FIRE STATION No. 6
534 East Edgeware Road, Los Angeles (original location at 1279 Temple Street). This Mediterranean masonry station was built in 1929, and moved to its present site in 1948.
Declared:11/1/1994 *(pg. 101)*

HCM #606
KERKHOFF HOUSE
734 West Adams Boulevard, Los Angeles. Designed in 1906 in the English Tudor style by architects Hunt & Eager, this mansion is now part of the University of Southern California campus.
Declared:11/1/1994 *(pg. 322)*

HCM #607
POWERS APARTMENT BUILDING #1
2327 Scarff Street, Los Angeles. Designed in the Prairie style, this apartment building, along with Buildings #2 and #3, was designed by George Wyman and built by contractor John Zeller for developer John Powers in 1908. The buildings comprise the Powers triptych streetscape.
Declared:11/1/1994 *(pg. 301)*

HCM #608
POWERS APARTMENT BUILDING #2
2326 Scarff Street, Los Angeles. Building #2 is notable for the influence of Beaux Arts Classicism, as evidenced by the balustraded balcony supported by the entrance columns.
Declared:11/1/1994 *(pg. 325)*

HCM #609
POWERS APARTMENT BUILDING #3
2310 Scarff Street, Los Angeles. The Prairie style form of Building #3 is altered by the addition of a Classical Revival entry featuring a broken pediment above the door.
Declared:11/1/1994 *(pg. 325)*

HCM #610
SHANKLAND HOUSE
715 West 28th Street, Los Angeles. Built in 1896 from a design by architects Eisen & Hunt, this Colonial Revival Foursquare house incorporates distinguishing characteristics, including a square plan, hip roof, semi-circular pediments and classically detailed, columned porticos with entablatures. The residence is now a fraternity house.
Declared:11/1/1994 *(pg. 334)*

HCM #611
MINSTER RESIDENCE
4163 Sea View Lane, Mt. Washington. Built in 1911, this Craftsman house was designed by Harry Grey.
Declared:11/8/1994 *(pg. 199)*

HCM #612
BIRTCHER-SHARE RESIDENCE
4234 Sea View Lane, Mt. Washington. Constructed in 1942, this International Style house was designed by architect Harwell Hamilton Harris.
Declared:11/8/1994 *(pg. 175)*

HCM #613
SCHOLFIELD HOUSE
4252 Sea View Lane, Mt. Washington. This structure was designed by James DeLong, a disciple of Frank Lloyd Wright. It was built in 1953 using Wright's Usonian principles.
Declared:11/8/1994 *(pg. 182)*

HCM #614
WOLFORD HOUSE
4260 Sea View Lane, Mt. Washington. Built in 1949, the house was designed by architect James DeLong. He incorporated many of Frank Lloyd Wright's Usonian principles including horizontal volumes, walls and glass surfaces in the same plane, hipped roof without parapets, extensive use of glass and a close relationship of interior and exterior spaces.
Declared:11/8/1994 *(pg. 172)*

HCM #615
SAN PEDRO FIRM BUILDING
108 North San Pedro Street, Los Angeles. Built in 1925 in the Classical Revival style from a design by William E. Young, it features a formal symmetrical façade, brick pilasters and the primary elevation organized into three horizontal zones (base, shaft and capital). The structure helps document the history of the Japanese American community in the first half of the 20th century and represents the mixed-use building of apartments over stores once prominent in Los Angeles.
Declared: 1/18/1995 *(pg. 65)*

HCM #616
THE TRIANON AND NEON ROOF SIGN
1750-1754 North Serrano Avenue, Los Angeles. Designed by Leland Bryant and erected in 1928, the six-story French Norman apartment building with its neon roof sign is distinguished by a round, conically roofed tower, a steep, hipped slate roof and dormers with narrow windows.
Declared: 6/23/1995 *(pg. 149)*

HCM #617
HOLLYWOOD PILGRIMAGE MEMORIAL MONUMENT
2580 Cahuenga Boulevard, Hollywood. The 32-foot-high steel cross was erected in 1923 and dedicated to the memory of Christine Witherall Stevenson, one of the founders of the Hollywood Bowl.
Declared: 7/25/1995 *(pg. 148)*

HCM #618
McDONNELL RESIDENCE / FOUNDER'S HOME: URBAN ACADEMY
601 North Wilcox Avenue, Los Angeles. Erected in 1920, this Mediterranean Revival single-family dwelling was built for the founder of Urban Military Academy, Mary McDonnell.
Declared:11/22/1995 *(pg. 405)*

HCM #619
WOLFF-FIFIELD HOUSE (exterior only)
111 North June Street, Los Angeles. Erected in 1929, the residence was designed in the Tudor Revival style. It the former home of Ralph Wolff, one of the pioneer financiers of Los Angeles, and later Reverend James Fifield, pastor of the First Congregational Church.
Declared: 1/9/1996 *(pg. 397)*

HCM #620
LEIMERT PLAZA
4395 Leimert Boulevard, Los Angeles. Built in 1928, the plaza is an excellent example of work by the Olmsted Brothers landscape firm. Its axial plan, described as Spanish Islamic, is symmetrical and includes a central fountain.
Declared: 2/2/1996 *(pg. 23)*

HCM #621
ALICE LYNCH RESIDENCE
2414 4th Avenue, Los Angeles. Erected in 1922 and designed by architect Harwood Hewitt, this single-family Spanish Colonial Revival adobe residence incorporates the distinguishing characteristics of a low gable roof, plaster walls, recessed windows, limited openings and decorative iron work.
Declared: 3/6/1996 *(pg. 331)*

HCM #622
TAFT HOUSE AND LANDSCAPING
16745 San Fernando Mission Boulevard, Granada Hills. Erected in the late 19th century, this Shingle style residence features wood siding and trim, shingled gambrel roof, double-hung windows, dormers and a wraparound porch supported by turned-wood columns.
Declared: 4/16/1996 *(pg. 235)*

HCM #623
KAPPE RESIDENCE
715 Brooktree Road, Pacific Palisades. Erected in 1967, this was the residence architect Ray Kappe designed for himself and his family. It includes the character-defining features of wood siding and trim, flat roofs, walls and fenestration in plane, expansive glass, horizontality, cantilevered volumes and open-plan interiors closely related to the outdoors.
Declared: 4/16/1996 *(pg. 366)*

HCM #624
LAWRENCE AND MARTHA JOSEPH RESIDENCE AND APARTMENTS
3819-3827 Dunn Drive, Los Angeles. Built and embellished by Lawrence Joseph from 1946 to 1970, the Storybook style apartment court incorporates the distinguishing characteristics of the idiom. Features include fanciful building shapes and roof forms, wood shingle siding, multi-paned fixed and casement wood windows, clinker brick chimneys, half-timbering, a tree trunk porch support, jungle-like landscaping and garden pools. Interiors are replete with nautically detailed carved wood beams, built-in furniture and pegged floors.
Declared: 4/16/1996 *(pg. 22)*

HCM #625
THOMAS BUTLER HENRY RESIDENCE
1400 South Manhattan Place, Los Angeles. Designed by the Althouse Brothers, this Mediterranean Colonial Revival structure was erected in 1911.
Declared: 6/21/1996 *(pg. 229)*

HCM #626
EYRAUD RESIDENCE
1326 South Manhattan Place, Los Angeles. Erected in 1908, this Craftsman style home was designed by John P. Krempel.
Declared: 6/21/1996 *(pg. 329)*

HCM #627
JOHN F. POWERS RESIDENCE
1547 South Manhattan Place, Los Angeles. Built in 1910, this Chateauesque structure was designed and built by the Althouse Brothers, central figures in early Los Angeles real estate development.
Declared: 6/21/1996 *(pg. 300)*

HCM #628
JACK DOYLE RESIDENCE
620 South Irving Boulevard, Los Angeles. Built in 1919, this Mediterranean residence was designed by D.S. Haag for Jack Doyle. Doyle was a local entrepreneur famous for, among other things, boxing promotion.
Declared: 6/21/1996 *(pg. 398)*

HCM #629
ADAMS RESIDENCE
7400 Tampa Avenue, Reseda. Designed by architect Lloyd Wright and owner-built in 1939, this tiny (26' x 26') Modern home was planned to suit the extremes of climate in the San Fernando Valley. Diagonal placement of the structure to the east-west line, combined with a swooping bat-wing roof and deep overhangs, controls heat and light. The open floor plan flows around a central fireplace.
Declared:10/4/1996 *(pg. 244)*

HCM #630
PIERSON RESIDENCE
3124 Belden Drive, Los Angeles. Erected in 1925, this Mediterranean Revival residence was designed by F. Pierpont Davis.
Declared:11/13/1996 *(pg. 151)*

HCM #631
BANKS-HUNTLEY BUILDING
634 South Spring Street, Los Angeles. Erected in 1930, this Art Deco structure was designed by architects John and Donald Parkinson.
Declared: 1/14/1997 *(pg. 67)*

HCM #632
GOLDENFELD HOUSE
810 Bramble Way, Los Angeles. Designed by architects A. Quincy Jones, Jr. and Whitney Smith, this Modern home was built in 1950. The residence features wide walls of glass, low gable roof and open rooms that flow into each other without floor-to-roof divisions.
Declared: 2/4/1997 *(pg. 374)*

HCM #633
HAAS HOUSE
12404 Rochedale Lane, Los Angeles. Designed by architects A. Quincy Jones, Jr. and Whitney Smith for a housing development in what is now Crestwood Hills, this Modern home was built in 1950.
Declared: 2/4/1997 *(pg. 367)*

HCM #634
KALMICK HOUSE
12327 Rochedale Lane, Los Angeles. This 1950 residence designed by architects A. Quincy Jones, Jr. and Whitney Smith typifies the single-story, informal room arrangement of modernist residential architecture.
Declared: 2/4/1997 *(pg. 369)*

HCM #635
WECKLER HOUSE
12434 Rochedale Lane, Los Angeles. A. Quincy Jones, Jr. and Whitney Smith designed this excellent example of post-and-beam construction that exemplifies the principles of the Case Study House Program in 1950.
Declared: 2/4/1997 *(pg. 363)*

HCM #636
C.A. FELLOWS RESIDENCE
1215 Westchester Place, Los Angeles. Erected in 1911, this Tudor Revival structure incorporates high intersecting gables, plaster and brick walls, multi-paned casement windows, arched entryway, half-timbering, front porch, tall chimney and informal gardens.
Declared: 3/18/1997 *(pg. 375)*

HCM #637
CAMPBELL DIVERTIMENTO FOUNTAIN
1150 Brooklawn Drive, Los Angeles. Designed by Mexican architect Luis Barragan, this fountain was built in 1996.
Declared: 3/18/1997 *(pg. 363)*

HCM #638
EL PARADISO
11468 Dona Cecilia Drive, Los Angeles. This Modern dwelling, with aluminum structural frame and supports, was built in 1964. It was designed by architect Raphael Soriano, a major contributor to the Modernist movement in Los Angeles.
Declared: 3/18/1997 *(pg. 232)*

HCM #639
RUSKIN ART CLUB
800 South Plymouth Boulevard, Los Angeles. This residence was built in 1922. Architect Frank Meline designed the structure in the Mission Revival and Spanish Colonial styles.
Declared: 3/18/1997 *(pg. 409)*

HCM #640
VDL RESEARCH HOUSE
2300 Silver Lake Boulevard, Silver Lake. This International Modern residence was designed by architect Richard J. Neutra. It was originally built in 1932 and reconstructed by Neutra and son Dion after fire destroyed it in 1963.
Declared: 3/18/1997 *(pg. 287)*

HCM #641
BRYNMOOR APARTMENTS NEON ROOF SIGN
432-436 South New Hampshire Avenue, Los Angeles. The sign is contemporary to this Tudor Revival structure that was erected in 1925.
Declared: 6/4/1997 *(pg. 392)*

HCM #642
EMBASSY APARTMENTS NEON ROOF SIGN
702-708 South Mariposa Avenue, Los Angeles. The sign is contemporary to this Mediterranean Revival structure that was erected in 1926.
Declared: 6/4/1997 *(pg. 401)*

HCM #643
SUPERBA APARTMENTS INCANDESCENT ROOF SIGN
335 South Berendo Street, Los Angeles. The sign is contemporary to this Italian Renaissance Revival structure that was erected in 1925.
Declared: 6/4/1997 *(pg. 394)*

HCM #644
STONE HOUSE
8642 Sunland Boulevard, Sun Valley. Built in 1925, this Craftsman house features rock walls, gabled roofs, arched window openings, square tower and a stone chimney.
Declared:12/19/1997 *(pg. 234)*

HCM #645
HARVESTER FARMS
(site and barn only)
22049 Devonshire Street, Chatsworth. Erected in the early 20th century, the complex of buildings evokes a rural farm atmosphere in the midst of what is now a suburban setting. The main house is a California Ranch structure. The California basilica-type barn still retains a high degree of original building fabric. This site was the headquarters of the Palomino Horse Association of America.
Declared:12/19/1997 *(pg. 251)*

HCM #646
VILLA SERRANO
930-940 South Serrano Avenue, Los Angeles. This French Norman Revival garden court apartment was built in 1936.
Declared:12/19/1997 *(pg. 393)*

HCM #647
STEN/FRENKE-GOULD RESIDENCE
126 Mabery Road, Los Angeles. Designed by architect Richard Neutra, this International Style residence was built in 1934.
Declared:12/19/1997 *(pg. 359)*

HCM #648
WITHERS RESIDENCE
2731 Woodshire Drive, Los Angeles. Architect L.A. Smith designed this Spanish Colonial Revival residence in 1926.
Declared:12/19/1997 *(pg. 150)*

HCM #649
CORA B. HENDERSON HOUSE
132 South Wilton Place, Los Angeles. This Craftsman residence was built in 1912.
Declared: 4/7/1998 *(pg. 394)*

HCM #650
MORTENSEN HOUSE
103 South Wilton Drive, Los Angeles. This Craftsman bungalow was built in 1913.
Declared: 4/7/1998 *(pg. 404)*

HCM #651
FILIPINO CHRISTIAN CHURCH
301 North Union Avenue, Los Angeles. This Gothic Revival church was erected in 1895.
Declared: 5/5/1998 *(pg. 64)*

HCM #652
JENSEN'S RECREATION CENTER AND ELECTRIC ROOF SIGN
1700 Sunset Boulevard, Los Angeles. Designed by architect E.E.B. Meinardus, this Beaux Arts and Italianate structure was built in 1924.
Declared: 9/18/1998 *(pg. 102)*

HCM #653
BRYSON APARTMENTS
2701 Wilshire Boulevard, Los Angeles. This ten-story Beaux Arts, Classical Revival and Mediterranean style building, which was designed by architects Frederick Noonan and Charles H. Kysor, was erected in 1912.
Declared: 9/18/1998 *(pg. 413)*

HCM #654
CRAFTSMAN MANSION
4318 Victoria Park Place, Los Angeles. This Craftsman house with Japanese and Swiss motifs was built in 1912.
Declared: 9/18/1998 *(pg. 339)*

HCM #655
GEORGE R. KRESS HOUSE
2337 Benedict Canyon Drive, Los Angeles. Architect Harry J. Muck designed this Tudor Revival residence for Kress. It was built in 1931.
Declared: 9/18/1998 *(pg. 372)*

HCM #656
BINOCULARS
340 Main Street, Venice. Erected in 1992, the four-story sculpture was designed by artists Claes Oldenburg and Coosje van Bruggen. The piece is an excellent example of the integration of art and architecture. It serves as the physical and visual gateway arch to the building and is the focal point of the main façade of the office development designed by Frank Gehry.
Declared:10/14/1998 *(pg. 22)*

HCM #657
LOS FELIZ HEIGHTS STEPS
Cromwell Avenue, Bonvue Avenue, Glencairn Road, Bryn Mawr Road and Glendower Avenue, Los Angeles. Built circa 1924, the steps include concrete fountains, benches, planters, retaining walls and metal rails.
Declared:10/14/1998 *(pg. 286)*

HCM #658
HARRY AND GRACE WURTZEL HOUSE
926 Longwood Avenue, Los Angeles. This Mediterranean residence was built in 1927.
Declared:11/4/1998 *(pg. 221)*

HCM #659
PACIFIC'S CINERAMA DOME THEATRE AND MARQUEE
6360 Sunset Boulevard, Hollywood. Architect Welton Becket designed this Modern structure. Built in 1963, this theater is the world's only example of a concrete geodesic dome.
Declared:12/18/1998 *(pg. 150)*

HCM #660
ROSENHEIM MANSION
1120 South Westchester Place, Los Angeles. Built in 1915 from a design by its owner, architect Alfred Rosenheim, the Tudor Revival house has brick and terra cotta cladding, leaded glass windows and a round stair tower.
Declared: 6/22/1999 *(pg. 335)*

HCM #661
RIVES MANSION
1130 South Westchester Place, Los Angeles. This brick Mediterranean residence with a clay tile roof has an elaborately-detailed interior including gold-leaf scrollwork, cast plaster, individualized fireplaces, a grand staircase, original light fixtures and stained glass.
Declared: 6/22/1999 *(pg. 309)*

HCM #662
PERRINE HOUSE
2229 South Gramercy Place, Los Angeles. Designed by architects Hunt & Eager, this Craftsman residence was built in 1908.
Declared: 6/22/1999 *(pg. 306)*

HCM #663
UPLIFTERS CLUBHOUSE
601 Latimer Road, Los Angeles. Architect William J. Dodd designed this Spanish Colonial Revival structure that was constructed in 1923.
Declared: 8/10/1999 *(pg. 378)*

HCM #664
BROADWAY DEPARTMENT STORE AND NEON SIGN
6300 Hollywood Boulevard, Hollywood. Architect Fred Dorn designed this Renaissance Revival structure that was erected in 1927.
Declared: 9/29/1999 *(pg. 152)*

HCM #665
HOLLYWOOD PLAZA HOTEL AND NEON SIGN
1633 Vine Street, Hollywood. Designed by architects Walker & Eisen, this Neo-Renaissance and Spanish Colonial Revival building was constructed in 1924.
Declared: 9/29/1999 *(pg. 152)*

HCM #666
TAFT BUILDING AND NEON SIGN
6280 Hollywood Boulevard, Hollywood. Architects Walker & Eisen designed this Neo-Renaissance style building, erected in 1923.
Declared: 9/29/1999 *(pg. 151)*

HCM #667
LEADER BUILDING'S ROOFTOP NEON SIGN
344-346 North Fairfax Avenue, Los Angeles. Installed in the mid-1940s, the three-sided sign spells "LEADER" in vertical block letters, and incorporates male and female heads outlined in neon tubing.
Declared: 9/29/1999 *(pg. 218)*

HCM #668
HILLSIDE HOUSE
8707 St. Ives Drive, Los Angeles. Built in 1962, this International Modern residence was designed by local architect Carl Maston.
Declared: 9/29/1999 *(pg. 368)*

HCM #669
BAILEY HOUSE (CASE STUDY HOUSE #21)
9038 Wonderland Park Avenue, Los Angeles. Designed by architect Pierre Koenig, this International Style residence was constructed in 1958.
Declared:11/9/1999 *(pg. 360)*

HCM #670
STAHL HOUSE (CASE STUDY HOUSE #22)
1635 Woods Drive, Los Angeles. Designed by architect Pierre Koenig and immortalized in Julius Shulman's nighttime photograph, this International Style residence was constructed in 1960.
Declared:11/9/1999 *(pg. 361)*

HCM #671
BARCLAY'S BANK
639-641 South Spring Street, Los Angeles. Built in 1919 to house the Los Angeles Stock Exchange, this thirteen story Beaux Arts building was designed by architects Morgan, Walls & Morgan.
Declared:11/9/1999 *(pg. 66)*

HCM #672
PERCY H. CLARK RESIDENCE
2639 South Van Buren Place, Los Angeles. This Craftsman residence was built in 1903 by real estate developer Percy Clark.
Declared:11/9/1999 *(pg. 315)*

HCM #673
THE OUTPOST II
1851 Outpost Drive, Hollywood. This Spanish Colonial Revival residence was built in 1929. It was originally the site of The Outpost, an adobe structure where the Treaty of Cahuenga was signed in 1847, marking an end to California's involvement in the Mexican War.
Declared:11/17/1999 *(pg. 158)*

HCM #674
JACOBSON HOUSE
4520 Dundee Drive, Los Feliz. Architect Edward H. Fickett designed this post-and-beam style residence built in 1966.
Declared: 2/25/2000 *(pg. 288)*

HCM #675
VILLA ELAINE
1241-1249 North Vine Street, Hollywood. Architect L.A. Smith designed this Spanish Revival apartment structure constructed in 1925. Artist Man Ray was a tenant in the building.
Declared: 2/25/2000 *(pg. 153)*

HCM #676
NEUTRA OFFICE BUILDING
2379 Glendale Boulevard, Silver Lake. This International Modern building was designed by architect Richard Neutra and constructed in 1951.
Declared: 4/25/2000 *(pg. 287)*

HCM #677
HORATIO COGSWELL HOUSE
1244 South Van Ness Avenue, Los Angeles. Built in 1911 by Horatio Cogswell, this Craftsman residence includes servants' quarters.
Declared: 4/25/2000 *(pg. 298)*

HCM #678
FURLONG HOUSE
2657 South Van Buren Place, Los Angeles. Los Angeles architect Frank Tyler designed this transitional Tudor Craftsman house built in 1910. Thomas Furlong, city clerk and treasurer of the City of Vernon from 1907 to 1950, occupied this residence from 1921 to 1958 with his family.
Declared: 4/25/2000 *(pg. 322)*

HCM #679
MAVERICK'S FLAT
4225 South Crenshaw Boulevard, Los Angeles. Architect H.C. Howard designed this irregular plan structure built in 1937. Maverick's Flat has been a cultural venue for 35 years, showcasing such groups as Rufus, The Fifth Dimension and Earth, Wind and Fire. An Arthur Murray Dance Studio was once housed in the building.
Declared: 4/25/2000 *(pg. 24)*

HCM #680
MUTUAL HOUSING ASSOCIATION SITE OFFICE
990 Hanley Avenue, Los Angeles. Built in 1948, this Modern residence was designed by A. Quincy Jones, Jr. and Whitney R. Smith.
Declared: 6/6/2000 *(pg. 384)*

HCM #681
SCHOTT HOUSE
907 Hanley Avenue, Los Angeles. This residence was designed by A. Quincy Jones, Jr. and Whitney R. Smith and built in 1948.
Declared: 6/14/2000 *(pg. 362)*

HCM #682
S.H. WOODRUFF RESIDENCE
3185 Durand Drive, Los Angeles. Architect John De Lario designed this Spanish Colonial Revival home built in 1925.
Declared: 6/14/2000 *(pg. 371)*

HCM #683
CHASE KNOLLS GARDEN APARTMENTS
13401 Riverside Drive, Sherman Oaks. Designed by architect Heth Wharton, this garden apartment complex was constructed between 1947 and 1949.
Declared: 7/11/2000 *(pg. 247)*

HCM #684
HEART HOUSE
112 North Harvard Boulevard, Los Angeles. This Craftsman residence was designed by John and Donald Parkinson and constructed in 1910.
Declared: 10/3/2000 *(pg. 402)*

HCM #685
PASCUAL MARQUEZ FAMILY CEMETERY
635 San Lorenzo Street, Los Angeles. Begun circa 1848, the cemetery is one of the oldest burial grounds in the city and received its last human remains in 1916. The family was an 18th century landholder in the Los Angeles. This site also includes a John Byers-designed adobe enclosure wall (circa 1926).
Declared: 10/17/2000 *(pg. 384)*

HCM #686
SUPERIOR OIL COMPANY BUILDING
550 South Flower Street, Los Angeles. Architect Claude Beelman designed the Corporate Modern style building erected in 1955.
Declared: 10/24/2000 *(pg. 66)*

HCM #687
TORNBORG HOUSE
1918 North Tamarind Avenue, Los Angeles. This Craftsman residence was built in 1908.
Declared: 10/24/2000 *(pg. 154)*

HCM #688
HOLIDAY BOWL (façade and architectural treatment of the restaurant/café)
3730 South Crenshaw Boulevard, Los Angeles. The firm of Ted R. Cooper Co., Inc. constructed this Googie Modern building that was built in 1957. This site is a culturally important sports and entertainment center closely associated with the history of the African Americans and Japanese Americans in Los Angeles.
Declared: 12/15/2000 *(pg. 20)*

HCM #689
PHILIP CHANDLER HOUSE
2531 North Catalina Street, Los Angeles. Built in 1936 for a member of the prominent Chandler family, this Tudor Revival residence was designed by architect Gerald Colcord.
Declared: 2/6/2001 *(pg. 158)*

HCM #690
ELLIOT HOUSE
4237 Newdale Drive, Los Angeles. Architect Rudolph M. Schindler designed this 1930 International Modern style building.
Declared: 2/6/2001 *(pg. 289)*

HCM #691
CARL C. WARDEN RESIDENCE
878 Rome Drive, Los Angeles. Architects Meyer & Holler designed this Prairie style residence that was constructed in 1910.
Declared: 3/23/2001 *(pg. 179)*

HCM #692
DAHLIA MOTORS BUILDING
1627 Colorado Boulevard, Eagle Rock. This Art Deco building was built in 1931.
Declared: 4/24/2001 *(pg. 190)*

HCM #693
ISRAEL HOUSE
914 Bluegrass Lane, Los Angeles. Architects A. Quincy Jones, Jr. and Frederick R. Emmons designed this Modern residence built circa 1950.
Declared: 4/24/2001 *(pg. 377)*

HCM #694
EMMONS HOUSE
661 Brooktree Lane, Santa Monica. Architect Frederick R. Emmons designed this Modern residence for himself and his family in 1954.
Declared: 4/24/2001 *(pg. 374)*

HCM #695
GROSS HOUSE
860 Hanley Avenue, Los Angeles. This 1950 Modern residence was designed by A. Quincy Jones, Jr., Whitney R. Smith and Edgardo Contini.
Declared: 4/24/2001 *(pg. 382)*

HCM #696
JONES AND EMMONS BUILDING
12248 Santa Monica Boulevard, Los Angeles. Built in 1954, this Modern building was designed by A. Quincy Jones, Jr. and Frederick R. Emmons. Designed to house the architects' offices, it utilizes the contemporary post-and-beam construction the firm was noted for.
Declared: 4/24/2001 *(pg. 381)*

HCM #697
KERMIN HOUSE
900 Stonehill Lane, Los Angeles. This Modern residence was designed by A. Quincy Jones, Jr., Whitney R. Smith and Edgardo Contini and built circa 1950. It was built as part of an effort by the Mutual Housing Association to provide large-scale affordable housing in California.
Declared: 4/24/2001 *(pg. 366)*

HCM #698
SHERWOOD HOUSE
947 Stonehill Lane, Los Angeles. This Modern residence was designed by A. Quincy Jones, Whitney R. Smith and Edgardo Contini and built circa 1950.
Declared: 4/24/2001 *(pg. 381)*

HCM #699
AUGUST HOUSE
1664 Maltman Avenue, Los Angeles. This Craftsman residence was built in 1913.
Declared: 7/20/2001 *(pg. 290)*

HCM #700
CANOGA PARK BRANCH LIBRARY
7260 Owensmouth Avenue, Canoga Park. Designed by architects Ralph Bowerman and Charles Hobson, this Modern structure was constructed in 1959.
Declared: 7/20/2001 *(pg. 254)*

Acknowledgments

LANDMARK L.A. is a project that began in 1962, when the Cultural Heritage Commission was formed, at a time when no one dreamed that a book would even be necessary to record designations. But from those first slim files to the well-documented ones that have been compiled in years hence, a book featuring all seven hundred Historic-Cultural Monuments has evolved. It is a tribute to those commissioners and City Council members who have supported preservation in Los Angeles. Without their diligent persistence, much of our cultural and historic heritage might be left only to memory.

The visual record of these landmarks is the work of many photographers. For some of the vintage photographs we can only be grateful to anonymous eyes behind the lenses. However, it is with sincere thanks that I acknowledge the work of those who could be identified including Julius Schulman whose commitment to documenting the architecture of Los Angeles is legendary, Tom Zimmerman for the compelling cover image of City Hall and the many other photos he provided, and Tom Meyer for filling gaps in our photographic archive. I would also like to thank Carolyn Cole of the Los Angeles Public Library for finding essential historic photographs that appear in this book.

The support of the Historic Preservation Division of the Cultural Affairs Department has been essential in bringing together the disparate pieces required for the creation of this book. I am indebted to my colleagues, Haroot Avanesian, Matthew G. Dillhoefer, Elizabeth Hair, Virginia Kazor and Marjorie Thayne. Their commitment to historic preservation is exemplary.

This book would not be what it is without the passion and guiding energy of Paddy Calistro of Angel City Press and the equally enthusiastic people she brought to the project. From the meticulous fact checking and attention to detail of Ailene Kanbe and Andrea Richardson, to Scott McAuley's flawless index, to the technical wizardry and cover design of Amy Inouye, it has been my pleasure to watch this talented group put this book together.

I am most grateful for the support of Cultural Affairs Department Historic Preservation Officer Jay Oren whose encouragement kept this project on track. His understanding of the time needed to bring it to press was essential to its success. Ardella Patterson was instrumental to making sense of seven hundred images and seven hundred historic entries; for that I thank her. Ray Beccaria, Charlie Fisher, Portia Lee, John Livzey, Don Phaneuf, Bill Ralph and Joe Pluciniczak at Malloy Lithography, Sandra Rivkin, and Darren Schenck of the USC-Doheny Library helped make this a reality.

Finally, LANDMARK L.A. would never have been published without the vision of Cultural Affairs Department General Manager Margie Johnson Reese whose commitment to historic preservation is reflected in deeds as well as words. This book is but one aspect of her allegiance to historic preservation in Los Angeles. For her generosity in presenting me with this project I am deeply grateful. I also thank Christopher Molinar for his constant encouragement and support.

Jeffrey Herr

Photo Credits

The City of Los Angeles Cultural Affairs Department gratefully acknowledges the following photographers and sources for permission to use their photographs in *LANDMARK L.A.* Photographs which carry a credit line are not listed here. Numbers listed below refer to the Historic-Cultural Monument number; photographs not listed here are the property of the Cultural Affairs Department. The Department regrets any omissions; oversights will be corrected in the forthcoming editions.

Peter Antheil: #266

Bill Aron: #359

Daniel Atyian: #508

T. L. Bancroft/Vanguard: #17, #18, #20

Thomas Bate: #699

B'Hend & Kaufman Archives: #472, #524

B'Hend & Kaufman Archives, Helgesen Collection: #584

Jesse Blackwell: #54

Bruce Boehner: #52, #73, #77, #78, #138, #160, #178, #183, #197, #264, #269, #271, #278, #288, #294, #298, #354-358, #398, #432, #449, #459, #523

John Bolton: #62, #130, #145, #194, #199, #201, #203, #227, #237, #257, #258, #301, #316, #317

Alan Braus: #255

M.J. Buerger: #531

Frank Cooper: #341, #450, #596

Stephen Courtney: #67, #83, #87, #88, #100, #113, #114, #120, #129, #169, #170, #173, #189, #191, #207, #215-222, #238, #244, #250, #267, #268, #272, #273, #295, #296, #300

Mason Dooley: #286

Beverly Duke: #93

Charles J. Fisher: #284, #539-541, #550, #554, #556, #558, #564, #565, #585, #612

Douglas Hill: #26, #60, #61, #153, #321, #322, #340, #345, #346, #350, #352, #385, #396, #399, #431, #434, #442, #457, #460, #496, #504, #522, #526, #538

Historical Collection, Title Insurance & Trust Co.: #5, #13

Holtwick: #186

Neil Jacobson: #674

Tom La Bonge: #150, #162, #164, #236

Don Lord: #41

C.J. McAvoy: #274

Thos. K. Meyer: #22, #49, #50, #55, #108, #135, #184, #245, #282, #283, #287, #557, #573, #681, #690, #691, #694, #698

Willie Middlebrook: #146, #187, #249

Denver Miller: #305

Ron Miller: #175

John Miller: #292

Jay Oren: #458, #605

Jan C. Perry: #658

Roxanne Quezada: #69, #82, #104, #121, #131, #144, #156, #157, #167, #200, #259, #262, #265, #289

Richard Risemberg: #338, #339, #366, #369-377, #380, #383, #384, #388, #393, #394, #402, #404, #411, #416, #443, #464, #468-470, #481, #483, #486, #492-494, #503, #529, #533, #536, #537, #542, #549, #562

Security Pacific National Bank Collection, Los Angeles Public Library: #4, #163, #171, #270, #306, #525

Julius Shulman: #1-3, #6-9, #12, #14, #16, #19, #21, #23, #24, #27-33, #35, #37-40, #42, #43, #45-47, #51, #53, #56-59, #64, #66, #68, #70-72, #74-76, #79, #80, #85, #86, #89-91, #95-97, #99, #101-103, #106, #122-125, #127, #136, #152, #174, #204, #207, #230, #275, #325, #381, #669, #670

Carlos von Frankenberg (Julius Shulman Assocs.): #109, #115, #116, #139, #140, #142, #143, #158, #165, #166, #206, #208, #209, #212, #223, #229, #240

Nancy Stanford: #94, #134, #154, #155, #193, #235, #246, #248, #251-253, #285, #291, #303, #414, #505, #509

Frank Taylor: #81

Ed Tavetian: #506

Mitzi Trumbo: #198

Charles Wharton: #320

"Dick" Whittington: #700

Luke Wynne: #648

Cha Xiong: #640

Tom Zimmerman: #63, #84, #111, #137, #150 (cover), #172, #177, #181, #182, #188, #224, #225, #239, #247, #254, #260, #277, #280, #311, #314, #323, #330, #332, #343, #349, #389-391, #395, #401, #422, #435, #439, #445, #447, #451, #455, #490, #514, #518, #520, #527, #528, #530, #532, #563, #566, #567, #574, #575, #577, #578, #580, #583, #586, #588-590, #592-594, #603, #604, #611, #613-617, #619, #620, #623, #624, #630, #631, #636, #641-644, #653, #657, #660, #661, #665, #666, #671-673, #680

This Index features references to page numbers and, in many cases, to Historic-Cultural Monument (HCM) designation numbers. Here, HCM numbers appear in red [and in brackets], referring readers to the monument entries listed in numerical order in Part 2 (pages 421-477).

Italianate [#21, #66, #89, #97, #98, #108, #397, #420, #507, #516, #528, #572, #603, #652]

Mayan [#12, #33, #149, #235, #247]

Mediterranean / Mediterranean Revival [#238, #257, #279, #280, #285, #303, #318, #324, #353, #360, #391, #438, #445, #452, #475, #485, #513, #538, #562, #571, #581, #583, #605, #618, #625, #628, #630, #642, #653, #658, #661]

Mission / Mission Revival [#90, #135, #182, #185, #204, #222, #269, #331, #400, #421, #432, #463, #496, #565, #579, #639]

Modern [#228, #325, #368, #381, #390, #521, #530, #563, #623, #629, #632, #633, #634, #635, #638, #640, #659, #668, #674, #676, #680, #681, #686, #690, #693, #694, #695, #696, #697, #698, #700]

Moderne [#56, #122, #138, #156, #170, #183, #205, #232, #259, #290, #332, #361, #566, #587]

Moorish [#91, #286, #397, #476, #491, 549]

Prairie [#395, #482, #550, #607, #609, #691]

Queen Anne [#40, #51, #74, #77, #78, #107, #108, #129, #142, #143, #144, #145, #157, #167, #190, #191, #207, #217, #219, #220, #221, #223, #227, #240, #241, #262, #295, #296, #333, #335, #399, #403, #407, #408, #409, #416, #431, #433, #466, #497, #498, #519, #541, #602]

Renaissance / Renaissance Revival [#28, #274, #282, #309, #342, #345, #346, #354, #355, #356, #359, #476, #492, #532, #559, #569, #575, #664, #665, #666]

Romanesque / Romanesque Revival [#66, #89, #91, #114, #125, #200, #209, #212, #236, #307, #341, #350]

Second Empire [#11]

Spanish / Spanish Revival [#136, #192, #214, #292, #311, #362, #397, #435, #488, #531, #675]

Spanish Colonial / Spanish Colonial Revival [#1, #127, #178, #224, #231, #239, #250, #252, #254, #257, #263, #268, #276, #283, #285, #293, #302, #308, #337, #363, #387, #426, #428, #440, #444, #446, #447, #452, #545, #546, #574, #589, #594, #604, #621, #639, #648, #663, #665, #673, #682, #704]

Spanish Renaissance / Spanish Renaissance Revival [#90, #280, #315, #331, #386, #476, #573, #580]

Storybook [#383, #552, #624]

Tudor / Tudor Revival [#81, #161, #226, #230, #287, #297, #327, #430, #456, #471, #482, #554, #606, #619, #636, #641, #655, #660, #678, #689]

Victorian [#16, #30, #65, #97, #98, #102, #103, #147, #206, #234, #272, #321, #350, #378, #474]